The Sex Trade

Series Editor: Cara Acred

Volume 246

Independence Educational Publishers

First published by Independence Educational Publishers

The Studio, High Green

Great Shelford

Cambridge CB22 5EG

England

© Independence 2013

British Library Cataloguing in Publication Data

The sex trade. -- (Issues ; 246)
1. Sex-oriented businesses. 2. Internet pornography.
I. Series
363.4'4-dc23

ISBN-13: 978 1 86168 648 0

Printed in Great Britain

MWL Print Group Ltd

Contents

Chapter 1: Pornography

Chapter 2: Prostitution & trafficking

Introduction

The Sex Trade is Volume 246 in the **ISSUES** series. The aim of the series is to offer current, diverse information about important issues in our world, from a UK perspective.

ABOUT THE SEX TRADE

With 61% of children aged seven to 16 in possession of a mobile phone that can access the Internet, many young teens are now stumbling across disturbing pornographic images. Even adults are frequently unaware that 20% of all pornography images online are of children. Would pornography lessons in school help to address the issue? What about other aspects of the sex trade? This book also explores prostitution and sex trafficking; highlighting the link between the two industries and considering topics such as the legalisation of prostitution and child sexual exploitation in the UK.

OUR SOURCES

Titles in the **ISSUES** series are designed to function as educational resource books, providing a balanced overview of a specific subject.

The information in our books is comprised of facts, articles and opinions from many different sources, including:

- Newspaper reports and opinion pieces
- Website factsheets
- Magazine and journal articles
- Statistics and surveys
- Government reports
- Literature from special interest groups

A NOTE ON CRITICAL EVALUATION

Because the information reprinted here is from a number of different sources, readers should bear in mind the origin of the text and whether the source is likely to have a particular bias when presenting information (or when conducting their research). It is hoped that, as you read about the many aspects of the issues explored in this book, you will critically evaluate the information presented.

It is important that you decide whether you are being presented with facts or opinions. Does the writer give a biased or unbiased report? If an opinion is being expressed, do you agree with the writer? Is there potential bias to the 'facts' or statistics behind an article?

ASSIGNMENTS

In the back of this book, you will find a selection of assignments designed to help you engage with the articles you have been reading and to explore your own opinions. Some tasks will take longer than others and there is a mixture of design, writing and research-based activities that you can complete alone or in a group.

FURTHER RESEARCH

At the end of each article we have listed its source and a website that you can visit if you would like to conduct your own research. Please remember to critically evaluate any sources that you consult and consider whether the information you are viewing is accurate and unbiased.

What is pornography?

Everything you need to know.

Pornography

Pornography is a picture, magazine, or video that is sexually explicit and is used for sexual satisfaction. It's normal for young people to be curious about sex, and some young people see porn as a way to learn more about sex.

The trouble is that pornography isn't real, it often gives the viewer a negative view of him/herself, and it can cause problems in real relationships.

Porn can lower self-esteem. In a survey for the Channel 4 *Sex Education vs. Pornography* programme, 60% of the teenagers interviewed said that viewing pornography affected their self-esteem and body image. 45% of young women said that they were unhappy with their breasts and would consider plastic surgery and 27% of young men were concerned about the shape and size of their penis.

The thing to remember is that many porn stars – and actors and models – have had plastic surgery and wear loads of make-up. Their photos are airbrushed and adjusted to make them look thinner and taller, their skin more wonderful and sometimes their breasts are enhanced. Often the picture in the magazine doesn't even look like the real person! Real people come in all shapes and sizes, and even models and porn stars find it hard to live up to the media's standards of beauty.

Many of the major faiths suggest that pornography is not appropriate.

Within Islam, porn is seen as fornication and is forbidden even in a person's own home. Sikhs avoid pornography because they believe that pornography can lead to lust (Kaam) – an unhealthy obsession with sex – which, in turn, creates a barrier between humanity and God. Similarly, many Christians see pornography as a sexual sin, one of the passages that is used to back up this opinion is, Matthew 5:28. Jesus said that 'anyone who looks at a woman lustfully has already committed adultery with her in his heart'.

Hindu texts, however, are less clear about whether or not pornography is sinful or not. The *Kama Sutra*, for example, is a guide to love and family life, including a section which has even been called a 'sex manual'. In addition, many Hindu temples have statues and carvings that can be described as sexually explicit. However, many Hindus believe that pornography has a negative effect on relationships. Hindus in Holland are fighting hard against a pornography organisation that uses the name of one of their gods to sanction pornography because they find it insulting to their religion and culture.

Porn ignores a lot of the good things about relationships and focuses on just one thing: sex. Sex between two people who love and care for each other can be a really fantastic way of deepening a relationship. Pornography takes the love and respect out of sex and ignores so many of the good things about relationships: fun, laughter,

security, a feeling of belonging, knowing and being completely known by another person. Instead it focuses on just sex, so that it seems like sex is the only thing that matters in a relationship.

Porn can damage the viewer's relationships with real people. Some people neglect their partners or don't develop healthy relationships in the first place because porn requires less time and effort than a real relationship. What these people don't realise is that the pleasures of pornography only last for that moment, while the pleasures of a deep and healthy relationship can last and grow for years. A video doesn't keep you warm at night or discuss your hopes and dreams for the future.

In some cases, porn can lead to abuse. Porn can be very violent, and then influence people so they think that sexual violence is okay. Also, someone who watches a lot of pornography may begin to think that people exist just for sex. This mindset makes it very difficult to have normal relationships with people.

Porn can make real sex less satisfying. When someone watches a lot of porn, he/she might think that all sexual experiences should be like the pornographic ones he/she has seen. With all these unrealistic expectations, real sex just doesn't seem all that exciting.

Pornography can be addictive. The first time a viewer watches porn, he/she may feel sexually aroused. With time, the viewer may need a more extreme or shocking form of pornography to get the same satisfaction as the first time. Other viewers will simply feel as though they cannot help looking at porn, and this may lead to feelings of guilt and shame.[1] An increasing tendency is to act out sexually the behaviours viewed in the pornography, including violence during sex. This behaviour frequently grew into a sexual addiction which they found themselves locked into and unable to change or reverse, no matter what the negative consequences were in their life.'

Porn can lead to feelings of guilt and shame. For many, especially those from faith backgrounds, porn can be seen as something bad that should be avoided. Many young people of faith have heard that porn is sinful, and a person can feel guilty very easily the first few times he/she looks at porn. However, he/she can become numb to their conscience, and then go from viewing soft porn to watching hard-core and even violent porn without really realising how that happened. Other viewers of pornography may feel helpless because they feel weighed down by guilt for looking at pornography, but cannot seem to stop.

What it all comes down to is that pornography can be damaging, really damaging. Pornography can damage a person's self-image and sense of worth, pornography can damage a person's relationships and long-term enjoyment of life, and pornography can, according to many of the major faiths, damage a person's spiritual wellbeing.

⇨ The above information is reprinted with kind permission from Faith Relationships & Young People (FRYP) website. Please visit www.fryp.org.uk for further information.

1   Cline, Victor B.. 'Pornography's Effects on Adults and Children'. http://mentalhealthlibrary.info/library/porn/pornlds/pornldsauthor/links/victorcline/porneffect.htm.

Porn – the reality behind the fantasy

The Women's Support Project sees pornography as a form of commercial sexual exploitation and part of the spectrum of violence against women.

Pornography is a multi-million pound industry and produces 68 million search engine requests each day.[1] It is now part of our popular culture, with images used in advertising, music videos and mainstream films and porn stars promoted as international celebrities. The porn industry produces more hard-core material that is both overtly cruel toward women and yet more widely accepted than ever. At the same time our culture denounces other forms of violence against women.

The dominant culture tries to justify pornography – saying that those who are anti-porn are somehow at fault, prudes, anti-sex, not 'getting the message' or just 'not with it'. This minimising of opposition acts as a silencing tactic and can deter people from becoming activists.

We have taken some commonly used arguments in favour of pornography and distinguished fact from fiction to support people taking action.

FICTION – it's just two people having sex

We want a culture where people are sexually healthy and free of exploitation, coercion and violence. Pornography is a harmful product, produced to make profit. Viewing or making it is not a form of sexual expression or sexual liberation. The pornography industry distorts our conceptions of sex and sexuality and portrays women and girls as sexual objects, turning their bodies into commodities to be bought, sold and marketed in whatever form will make the most profit. The majority of mainstream pornography now

1   Internet Filter Review, top ten reviews

contains extreme levels of violence, with almost all of this violence directed at women by men. This links violence with sexual arousal and can encourage men to think their arousal is mirrored in all women. Porn caters to and reflects this privilege back at men, creating and supporting a vicious circle. This narrow depiction of sexuality has now been normalised and is becoming more and more part of how the mainstream media depicts women.

FACT

One study examined 304 scenes from the most popular adult videos released in 2005 in the US. They found that 89.8% of the scenes included either verbal or physical aggression. 48% contained verbal aggression, mostly name-calling and insults, while 82.2% contained physical aggression. 94.4% of the aggressive acts were targeted at women.

(Robert Wosnitzer, Ana Bridges & Michelle Change (2008) 'Mapping the Pornographic Text: Content Analysis Research of Popular Pornography')

FICTION – if you are anti-porn then you are anti-sex

We believe in sexual freedom for all people based on equality and consent. Pornography is not about sex – it is a medium that uses sexual activity to sell its products. Porn often portrays women-hating and violent misogynistic acts. Sex is about more than this disconnected narrow definition and understanding of sexuality. Sex can be about humanity, connection, tenderness, love and respect for the other. The prevalence of these images impacts on how society, and particularly young people, view women and sexual relationships. In a society where one in four women will experience violence and where there is a rape conviction rate of under 4%, the widespread availability of these images reinforces the attitudes that fuel this inequality.

FACT

In a study conducted by Malmuth, participants were exposed to less than five hours of pornography over a six-week period. This resulted in participants showing much more lenient attitudes towards rapists.

(Malamuth & Donnerstein, Pornography and Sexual Aggression, 1984)

FICTION – women get paid and choose to be in porn, they are not being exploited

Yes, some people do choose to enter the porn industry and publicly endorse it, typically saying they do it because they love sex, because they feel good about their bodies, because it makes them feel powerful and liberated. It's important to remember that these women are 'on the job', marketing for the industry. The average career span of a female performer is around a year having made just four or five[2] films and upward career progress in the industry is rarer for women than men.

The empowerment for women involved is then questionable. Receiving payment is not a good indicator of whether someone is being exploited. 'Glamourising' the industry and focusing on the lavish lifestyles of its members supports the myth of 'easy money'. Feminists recognise that women may choose to enter the industry but do not then choose the conditions under which they work. Women working in the porn industry have very few employment rights and they are often coerced into breaking their boundaries and taking part in more body punishing sex in order to produce more extreme images. Studies consistently show that high numbers of women in the

porn industry have experienced sexual abuse as children or young adults, poverty, homelessness and substance misuse. As in other areas of the sex industry, it is the people who buy, produce and control the porn industry who are making choices.

FACT

Chlamydia and Gonorrhea infections among performers are 10 times greater than that of ordinary 20–24 year olds. The risk and burden of sexually transmitted infections among porn performers are unacceptably high.

(Los Angeles Public Health Department)

FICTION – you can't ban porn, that's censorship!

We favour education, awareness-raising, public forums and discussions with a human rights approach as more appropriate ways to challenge these misrepresentations. No one has the right to exploit or sell women's bodies but many assume they have that privilege and entitlement. We believe in freedom of expression but this should not be at the cost of the human rights of women to be free from degrading and inhumane treatment. The notion of freedom of expression is exploited by pornographers as a way of justifying and profiting from violence against women.

FACT

The United Nations Special Rapporteur on violence against women, its causes and consequences, specifically noted pornography in a report for the UN Human Rights Commission stating that it 'glamorises the degradation and maltreatment of women and asserts their subordinate function as mere receptacles for male lust'.

(Radhika Coomaraswamy (1994) www1.umn.edu/humanrts/ commission/thematic51/42.htm)

FICTION – porn is harmless entertainment for adults

Porn is exploitation, not entertainment. It is mainly accessed via the Internet

which is an extremely easy and cheap way to distribute porn and as a result the content has become ever more extreme to compete with rapidly increasing demand. You can access extreme images depicting rape and violence in just two clicks from a search engine. This content is often free, anonymous and easily available but this does not mean it is harmless for those who are expected to endure more extreme sex, those who are aroused by it or for women and children in general. Age verification systems are not used and young people can access it both intentionally and inadvertently.

FACT

42% of a nationally representative sample of 1,500 Internet users in the US aged ten to 17 had been exposed to pornography in the last year, with two-thirds reporting only unwanted exposure. The research also found an increase in unwanted exposure from 26% between 1999 and 2000, to 34% in 2005.

(Wolak, Mitchell & Finkelhor, 2007: 247–257)

⇨ The above information is reprinted with kind permission from Women's Support Project. Please visit www. womenssupportproject.co.uk for further information.

2 Fornander, Kjell (July 1992). 'A Star is Porn'. *Tokyo Journal*. Archived from the original on 2006-05-16.

© Women's Support Project 2013

Can sex films empower women?

Following former Home Secretary Jacqui Smith's BBC Radio 5 documentary about pornography, Gail Dines, sociologist and author, debates the issue with Anna Arrowsmith, a pornographic film-maker and former LibDem candidate.

By Emine Saner

Former Home Secretary Jacqui Smith this week reopened the debate about the impact of the sex industry on society with her BBC Radio 5 documentary about pornography. Here, Gail Dines, Professor of Sociology and Women's Studies at Wheelock College in Boston, and author of *Pornland: How Porn Has Hijacked Our Sexuality*, and Anna Arrowsmith, a former Liberal Democrat candidate who makes pornographic films under the name Anna Span, discuss the issues. Emine Saner listens in.

Gail Dines: I'm concerned about what it means to live in a society that is overwhelmed by images created by predatory capitalists whose job is to maximise profits. Pornography is the commodification of sexuality and the product is plasticised and lacks any individuality. My feeling is that you're talking from a more personal perspective, and there are certainly ways in which some women can make pornography work for them. My issue is beyond you and me, and into a more political analysis of what it means to live in a society where women are systematically discriminated against, and then have a juggernaut called pornography shaping the way men think about us – the same men who go on to make laws and policy that impact on the lives of women.

Anna Arrowsmith: I used to be anti-pornography until I realised my anger was jealousy – I was envious of men having their sexuality catered for. I realised the best thing I could do was to work towards women learning their own sexual identity. I'm not just coming from a personal experience – I've been chair of the Adult Industry Trade Association in the UK. We don't get well represented in the media, we're a soft target, using moral panics to say we're the devil, and that if you

just get rid of pornography, amazingly women will get full equality.

GD: I understand being envious of men's sexual freedom, but the bigger point is that men have too much economic and cultural power, and women making pornography is not going to change that. If we want equality, we will have to do it on the political and economic level, and making porn is a trivial response.

AA: The anti-porn stance encourages women to think of themselves as victims.

GD: How?

AA: You don't allow women the individual choice to opt in.

GD: Of course individual women can be empowered – I'm extremely empowered in my life, but just because I, as a white, middle-class educated woman, am empowered does not mean we have women's liberation. It means I have a duty to use my privilege to fight for women who are discriminated against.

AA: So do I, and that's why I fight against people who argue against women in the sex industry. We get a lot of aggression from people like you and it's important that empowered women like myself stand up for porn stars and say, please listen to them. If they say they are happy, please respect their autonomy.

GD: Women who work in the sex industry and promote this in the name of feminism are the scabs of the feminist movement. I think you are an apologist, and selling women out.

AA: I'm not an apologist. I'm here because women want sexuality to be represented. If you hand over all sexual imagery to men, you hand over that power. I'm not saying all pornography is positive to women, but the only way

you are going to change that is from working with the images themselves.

GD: We know that most women leave the porn industry with barely the clothes on their backs, they do not leave with millions of dollars. This industry is based on poor women who have few economic choices. Pornography is promoted as a way to economic empowerment, and that's a lie.

AA: I wouldn't disagree that women have bad experiences after [leaving the porn industry], but that is because society has such a bad attitude towards people who work in the sex industry. That's the attitude of the mainstream media and the culture we live in who don't respect sex workers as equals.

GD: I would put the stigma on the users and the men who buy sex. I am for women thinking about images of sexuality, but it's a joke if you think you are going to do it within this predatory capitalist industry. I went on your website and it looks like any other porno website – what are you doing that is different from what every other pornographer is doing?

AA: You haven't seen my films. An important part of them is the development of character and plot, and the role women play in the film. Women have an opportunity now to express their sexuality. Anyone can get a webcam and go on the Internet, it has turned into a massive cottage industry, and that is an incredibly democratic move.

GD: Anyone can get an allotment and grow their own food – but the reality is that the food industry is run by agrobusiness, and the porn industry is run by the mega porn businesses. With all due respect, you are not shaping male sexuality on a macro level.

AA: You insult us alternative porn makers. I've had a huge effect in the industry, in how women are perceived in films and how men now direct in the UK. I've also changed stylistically and creatively how porn films are made in the UK. You will see a lot more camera angles looking at the man [from a female point of view], and that is because I worked within the industry and I changed it. Women need a voice against women like you to stand up and say I'm not a victim. You need to talk to porn stars ...

GD: Porn stars? Do you know how many 'porn stars' there are? The vast majority of women I've talked to [in the industry] are not porn stars, they last three to five months, and leave with very little money. That's the way people coming from your position misrepresent the lives of women in the industry. The vast majority do not become 'stars'. Having more women in the industry is a cop-out.

AA: I can tell you that from watching pornography I have learned more about my own sexuality. It was my first instance of having an orgasm, and a lot of women learn that through pornography.

GD: This is not about you, this is about a huge industry that is having an enormous cultural impact. We have a right as a culture to define an authentic sexuality that grows out of people's experiences, desires, sexual needs and wants. What we've got instead is a generic, formulaic sexuality that comes out of an industry. That's what industries do. To think that you can work in an industry and somehow change it, that's a naive view of how capitalism works.

5 March 2011

The article originally appeared in *The Guardian* and is reprinted with permission. Please visit www.guardian.co.uk for further information.

LA County introduces condom law for porn films

In November 2012, Measure B (the 'Safer Sex in the Adult Film Industry Act') was passed by voters in LA County. The law requires all porn actors to wear condoms and was widely protested by the adult film industry. In order to legally film explicit sex scenes, porn producers in LA County must now apply for a permit from the County's Department of Public Health. So far this year, only two permits have been issued. Prior to the introduction of Measure B, approximately 500 permits were issued annually - leading to speculation that the new law is causing adult film companies to move their production elsewhere.

Diane Duke, chief executive of the Free Speech Coalition, a porn industry trade group, said that the drop in permit applications was to be expected because consumers want to see scenes without condoms. She added that many porn producers are currently suspending production while they await the outcome of a lawsuit that challenges Measure B on the grounds of breaching freedom of speech.

Michael Weinstein, president of the AIDS Healthcare Foundation, strongly supported the introduction of Measure B and claims that there is no evidence that the industry is filming elsewhere. However, Ventura Country Supervisor Linda Parks says that since the new law passed in November there has been a steep increase in phone calls from constituents who are upset by the filming of sex scenes in their area. Tim Gray, a 56-year-old father of four said 'It's really disturbing... we heard these loud sounds outside, like something really bad had happened. I went outside and heard, well the typical sounds you'd hear in a porn movie. It was echoing all over the neighborhood. Later I asked my daughter if she heard it. She said, "Yeah, I was doing my homework and I just turned up the music to down it out."'

Assemblyman Isadore Hall III has now proposed a bill modeled on Measure B that would extend the law to cover the entire state of California.

14 April 2013

⇨ The above article was written by Cara Acred, on behalf of Independence Educational Publishers.

How good is porn?

By Lucy Uprichard

In January 2013, Diane Abbott raised concerns about what she referred to as an 'increasingly pornified' youth culture in Britain and advised parents to talk more with their children about sexuality and its place in modern culture. This, perhaps, is not a conversation that should be exclusively for young people, but one that we should all be having. How much do we really know about porn and its impact on modern living?

The Internet has more or less revolutionised the way porn can be accessed. It's often said that half of the Internet is pornographic images. That isn't true (it's really more like 4%) but it can seem that we are subjected to a disproportionate number of sexual images every day, particularly in the form of pop-up ads. I once spent a week keeping a record of the number of advertisements for porn that I came across in normal Internet browsing and ended up with a tally of around 20. Some were obviously more explicit than others, but even the tamest seemed to suggest a degree of objectifying fantasy bordering on the comical – I simply refuse to believe that there are that many hot singles in my area. We are so used to seeing overtly sexual images in our daily lives that we become almost desensitised to it. That's where 'How Good Is Porn' comes in.

"The Internet has more or less revolutionised the way porn can be accessed"

I found out about HGIP through a flyer in a collection of Manchester circulars. Its design is deliberately striking and the lack of information bar the web address cannot fail to capture at least momentary attention. Logging onto the site takes you to a short anonymous survey with questions such as 'porn stars are lucky, loaded and love it – agree/disagree'. Answering them redirects to a page that gives you some quotes and statistics in regards to the true nature of porn. Without revealing all the answers here, I think it's safe to say that some of the numbers are, to say the least, shocking. I for one certainly didn't know that 20% of all pornographic images online are of children.

"There are real dangers in the world of prostitution and porn that cannot be ignored"

At the end of the survey there is an option to give feedback, through which I attempted to get in contact with the creators in the hope of discovering more about who they are. In response I received an email telling me that HGIP is run by an group of creatives and campaigners 'who for various reasons have become concerned about the negative impact of porn'. They likened the porn problem to 'an Emperor's New Clothes thing ... we are simply hoping to be the little kid who points and says 'anyone noticed what is going on here?'' Preferring to remain anonymous so that 'people will focus on the cause rather than us', the people behind HGIP are concerned about raising awareness about porn and its unspoken underlying issues.

If nothing else, the HGIP project forces you to reassess exactly how much of a growing concern porn is. Everybody knows at the very back of their minds that so much of pornography is morally questionable to say the least, but we rarely mention it or act upon it. There is a misconception in some feminist circles that porn is just another form of sexual freedom that should be tolerated without comment. This shouldn't be the case – if there is an area where we should be as critical as possible it is sex work. Romanticised images of Billie Piper in *Secret Diary of a Call Girl* aside, there are real dangers in the world of prostitution and porn that cannot be ignored, and the How Good Is Porn project is one small step towards bringing these into the public consciousness.

The people running HGIP told me that this campaign is just the beginning of a few things they are intending to do to 'get people thinking'. I don't know how widespread the campaign is, or whether it is localised to Manchester, but I'll be sure to keep an eye out. In the meantime, I urge all who read this to visit the site and share it around. Let's start a national dialogue about porn.

23 January 2013

⇨ The above article originally appeared in *The Huffington Post* and is reprinted with kind permission from AOL (UK). Please visit www.huffingtonpost.co.uk for further information.

Will UK law regarding online pornography be tightened?

By Tara Doyle

In December 2012, the Prime Minister David Cameron announced that children in the UK will be protected by an automatic block regarding online pornography, which parents must choose to have lifted.

This development comes after *The Telegraph* reported that the Government had decided against anti-pornography filters for the Internet, because such a system 'could create a false sense of security', meaning that parents might stop invigilating their children's Internet usage.

However, the Prime Minister has made clear his personal views in a statement to *The Daily Mail*. It seems he has taken notice of the fact that there are many reputable groups in favour of greater child protection from pornography on the Internet; for example, the Mothers' Union, the charity ChildLine and the NSPCC.

Additionally, Claire Perry, the Conservative MP for Devizes, handed a petition of 115,000 names into Downing Street in September. The petition demanded an automatic block on adult material for all Internet users; the so-called 'opt-in' system.

The new proposals from Cameron do not go this far; instead he has appointed Perry to be in charge of implementing a new web filter system, which will require Internet providers to check the age of the person setting controls.

The Mail reports that Internet providers will be required to produce plans by February 2013, detailing how they will ensure all parents are given the option of imposing filters on their home computers.

The Prime Minister claims that, once these controls are up and running, Great Britain will have the most robust protection for children against online pornography in the world.

The Mail points out, however, that concern remains about how the Government plans to address children accessing porn via smartphones.

While most people would agree it is desirable that children should be protected from pornography on the Internet, should there be an 'opt-in' system also for adults who wish to view explicit material in their homes?

As it happens, there is no legal definition of 'pornography', even with material in which sexual acts depicted are real rather than simulated. However, under the Obscene Publications Act 1959 (OPA), pornography is considered to be legally obscene if it has a tendency to 'deprave and corrupt' its audience.

The OPA is intended for use against publishers of extreme pornography, rather than against consumers. Nevertheless, much of this material is distributed from foreign websites, which may be out of reach for the British justice system.

The OPA is famous as the law under which the *Lady Chatterly's Lover* book trial took place in 1960, but it has since been amended to deal with electronically stored data or the transmission of such data. Notably, the issue of whether the material in question is obscene or not is generally decided by a jury.

However, there are changing attitudes to pornographic images, particularly since depictions of sado-masochism and bondage have entered mainstream popular culture, and this has meant that few cases are brought regarding obscene publications.

For example, in January 2012, the BBC reported that Michael Peacock, 53, was found not guilty by a jury at Southwark Crown Court, of six counts under the OPA. He had been accused of publishing DVDs for gay clients depicting 'hard-core' sexual acts, some involving urination. However, the jury found that the people seeking out such material

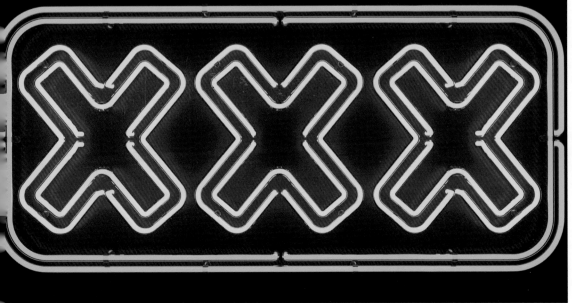

were not likely to become 'depraved or corrupt' after viewing it.

In contrast, Sections 63 to 67 of the Criminal Justice and Immigration Act 2008 concern the possession of extreme sexual images by Internet users. The Act makes it an offence to possess pornographic images that depict acts which threaten a person's life, acts which result in or are likely to result in serious injury to a person's anus, breasts or genitals; as well as bestiality or necrophilia. The maximum sentence upon conviction is three years imprisonment.

This law was brought in after a particularly shocking case, in which one Graham Coutts was accused of strangling and raping a schoolteacher, Jane Longhurst, in 2003. Coutts was also accused of storing her body for nefarious purposes before setting it alight several weeks after her death. The trial heard that Coutts had an addiction to extreme Internet pornography sites, which dwelt on subjects such as strangulation, rape and necrophilia.

The new law came into effect in 2009; but again, few cases have been prosecuted as the police do not actively seek out members of the public who view such material. This is in contrast to the way police investigate the possession of child sexual abuse images, with Child Exploitation and Online Protection officers in London monitoring file-sharing websites to search for individuals accessing such illegal material.

Reliable statistics regarding whether extreme pornography is a contributing factor to violent sexual crime are hard to come by, and academic studies on the matter appear to have widely varying conclusions.

There are those concerned with civil freedoms who argue that there should be no censorship on what adults choose to view in private; in contrast, there are many feminist and family-centred groups who argue that pornography of any type is a contributing factor to male aggression against women, as well as a significant factor in relationship breakdowns.

It would be interesting to see the reaction of public opinion if the Government mooted a change in the law that put in place an 'opt-in' system for all Internet users regarding pornography. This would be tantamount to expecting an adult to signal to their Internet provider that they wish to watch explicit material at home, and this might be considered an invasion of privacy.

On the other hand, the Government's proposed Data Communications Bill, which aims to allow the authorities access to a year's record of every citizen's Internet use on request, could accomplish a monitoring of pornography viewing habits.

However, this Bill has been widely labelled as a 'Snooper's Charter' and the Parliamentary Joint Committee on the draft Bill, as well as Internet service providers, have said the plans are unwieldy, as reported by *The Telegraph*.

It seems that adult Britons will continue to self-police their Internet use with regard to pornography, unless further shocking cases of sexual violence change public opinion. In the meantime, the Internet Watch Foundation, a self-regulatory body set up by Internet providers, provides a hotline for the public to confidentially report criminal online content that they may come across inadvertently.

21 December 2012

⇨ The above information is reprinted with kind permission from Contact Law. Please visit www.contactlaw.co.uk for further information.

© Contact Law

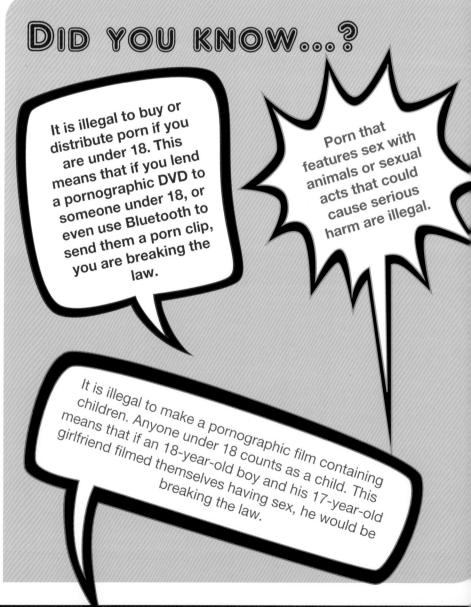

DID YOU KNOW...?

It is illegal to buy or distribute porn if you are under 18. This means that if you lend a pornographic DVD to someone under 18, or even use Bluetooth to send them a porn clip, you are breaking the law.

Porn that features sex with animals or sexual acts that could cause serious harm are illegal.

It is illegal to make a pornographic film containing children. Anyone under 18 counts as a child. This means that if an 18-year-old boy and his 17-year-old girlfriend filmed themselves having sex, he would be breaking the law.

Legal status of child pornography by country

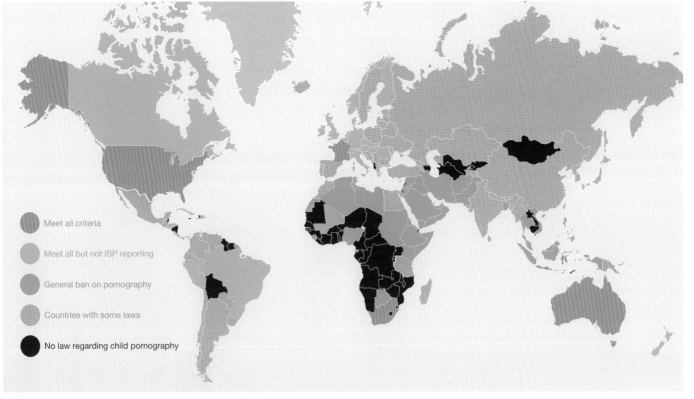

Legend:
- Meet all criteria
- Meet all but not ISP reporting
- General ban on pornography
- Countries with some laws
- No law regarding child pornography

This map shows legal status of child pornography. Child pornography refers to images or films (also known as child abuse images) and in some cases writings depicting sexually explicit activities involving a child; as such, child pornography is a record of child sexual abuse. Abuse of the child occurs during the sexual acts which are recorded in the production of child pornography, and the effects of the abuse on the child (and continuing into maturity) are compounded by the wide distribution and lasting availability of photographs of the abuse.

The laws of each country were assessed based on five criteria:

1. Are there existing laws criminalising child pornography?[1]

2. Does existing law include a legal definition of child pornography?

3. Is the possession of child pornography a crime?[2]

4. Is the distribution of child pornography via computer and the Internet a crime?[3]

5. Are Internet Service Providers (ISPs) required to report suspected child pornography to law enforcement?[4]

Number of countries meeting all of the criteria: 5

Number of countries meeting all but the last criteria, pertaining to ISP reporting: 24

Number of countries that do have some legislation specifically addressing child pornography: 68

Number of countries that have no legislation at all that specifically addresses child pornography: 92

1 Countries in which there is a general ban on pornography, regardless of whether the individuals being depicted are adults or children, are not considered to have 'legislation specific to child pornography', unless there is a sentencing enhancement provided for offences committed against a child victim.

2 Simple possession, refers to possession regardless of the intent to distribute.

3 Law mention of a computer, computer system, Internet, or similar language (even if such mention is of a 'computer image' or something similar in the definition of 'child pornography'). In cases where other language is used in national legislation, an explanatory footnote is provided.

4 While some countries may have general reporting laws (i.e. anyone with knowledge of any crime must report the crime to the appropriate authorities), only those countries that specifically require ISPs to report suspected child pornography to law enforcement (or another mandated agency) are included as having ISP reporting laws. Note that there are also provisions in some national laws (mostly within the European Union) that limit ISP liability as long as an ISP removes illegal content once it learns of its presence; however, such legislation is not included in this section.

Sources

INTERPOL 2007, Legislation of INTERPOL member states on sexual offences against children, 2007, INTERPOL, France, viewed 2nd June, 2010, <http://www.interpol.int/public/children/sexualabuse/nationallaws/default.asp>.

ICMEC 2008, Child Pornography: Model Legislation & Global Review, 5th Edition, International Centre for Missing & Exploited Children, Virginia, United States of America, viewed 2nd June, 2010, <http://www.icmec.org/en_X1/English__5th_Edition_.pdf>.

⇨ The above information is reprinted with kind permission from ChartsBin. Please visit www.chartsbin.com/view/q4y for further information.

© ChartsBin.com 2013

Citation: ChartsBin statistics collector team 2010, Legal Status of Child Pornography by Country, ChartsBin.com, viewed 1st February, 2013, <http://chartsbin.com/view/q4y>.

Children being exposed to pornography

Internet service providers could solve the problem by blocking pornography at network level whilst giving adults a choice to 'opt-in' to this content.

The issue

Every day children and young people are accessing mainstream pornography on the Internet, including the most hard-core, violent and abusive images. Evidence clearly shows pornography has a detrimental impact on children and young people including premature sexualisation, negative body image and unhealthy notions about relationships. This cannot be allowed to continue.

Despite parental concerns and the use of computer filters in the home, the rapid rate at which communications technology is developing, including convergence of the Internet on televisions/games consoles and mobile phone technology, makes it increasingly difficult for parents/carers to supervise their children's use effectively. Massive profit-driven competition is harming the vulnerable.

To better protect children and young people we are calling on Internet service providers to block pornography by introducing filters at Internet service provider level. This will still give adults the choice to access pornography whilst giving children the freedom to surf the Internet safely.

Key facts

Internet becoming integral part of family life in the UK

⇨ Approximately 73% of British households now have access to the Internet (ONS - Internet Access, August 2010).

⇨ 99% of 12- to 15-year-olds, 93% of 8- 11-year-olds, and 75% of 5- 7-year-olds use the Internet regularly (Ofcom, March 2010). In fact, 74% of 5- 16-year-olds have their own laptop or PC; almost 58% of 5- 16-year-olds can now access the Internet in their own room (ChildWise Monitor 2012).

⇨ Internet controls or filtering software is in place in only 39% of households where a child aged 5–15 uses the Internet at home (Ofcom 'Children and parents: media use and attitudes report' – October 2011).

Children and young people accessing pornography at an alarming rate

⇨ The single largest group of Internet pornography consumers is children aged 12–17 (*Psychologies Magazine*).

⇨ One in three ten year olds have seen pornography online (*Psychologies Magazine, 2010*).

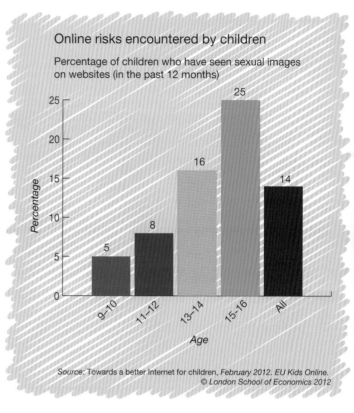

Online risks encountered by children

Percentage of children who have seen sexual images on websites (in the past 12 months)

Source: Towards a better Internet for children, *February 2012. EU Kids Online.*
© London School of Economics 2012

⇨ 81% aged 14–16 regularly access explicit photographs and footage on their home computers. (*Psychologies Magazine*, 2010).

Harmful impact of pornography on children and young people

Dr Linda Papadopolous, 'The evidence gathered in the review suggests a clear link between consumption of sexualised images, a tendency to view women as objects and the acceptance of aggressive attitudes and behaviour as the norm.' (Home Office report into the sexualisation of children 2010).

John Carr, Children's Charities Coalition on Internet Safety, 'In recent years there has been a very dramatic increase in child pornography images made by children and then distributed online or via phones. We have an exhibitionist, celebrity-dominated culture and it's seen as normal and cool to be a porn star.' (*Stella* magazine).

Author Mark Kastlemann said, 'Giving porn to a teenage boy is like giving crack to a baby. Addiction is almost guaranteed. No wonder boys aged 12–17 are the porn industry's core target.'

'Overall, the body of research on pornography reveals that pornography functions as a teacher, permission-giver and a trigger of negative behaviours and attitudes. The damage is seen in men, women and children, and to both married and single adults pathological behaviours, illegal behaviours and some behaviours that are both illegal and pathological.' (Mary Anne Layden, Director of Sexual Trauma and Psychological Program, University of Pennsylvania 2010).

'Studies cite alarming links between early exposure to pornography and juvenile sex offenders; one study of 30 young sex offenders showed that 29 had been watching X-rated porn from the age of seven.' (Sunday Telegraph *Stella* magazine, 27 November 2011).

Facts about the pornography industry and Internet service providers

⇨ The pornography industry was worth $96 billion (£61 billion) in 2006 (reference – '*Pornland*'). In the UK alone, it is estimated to be worth £1 billion (Adult Industry Trade Association – 2005).

⇨ One of the aims of the porn trade summit, XBIZ EU (2), held in London in September 2011 was 'to monetise the expanding audience of mobile users'.

⇨ The top six UK Internet Service Providers (all UK-based) account for over 90% of market share. Yet, only one of them, TalkTalk, is willing to block pornographic content at network level, although the default setting is still on, despite the technology being available to do so.

The problem with mobile phones

⇨ 61% of children aged 7–16 have a mobile phone that can access the Internet, rising to 77% among 11–16s (ChildWise Monitor 2012).

⇨ Nearly nine out of ten children had no security settings on their phones and only 46% of parents were aware that they were even necessary (YouGov Carphone Warehouse Jan 12).

⇨ Sexting – 40% of 11- to 14-year-olds have used their mobile phones or computer to send pictures of themselves or receive naked or topless images of friends (SW Grid for Learning Mar 11).

Pornography has detrimental impact on relationships and the family

⇨ Counsellors working for Relate report that use of Internet porn is a cause of tension and conflict for as many as 40% of their clients who come to them seeking help with sexual problems. Referrals to the Portman Clinic for the problematic use of pornography have increased from 9% in 2001–2002 to 16% in 2007–2008.

⇨ General public agree pornography is harmful to society.

⇨ A YouGov poll in February 2011 found that 93% of women and 73% men (83% average total) felt that the ease with which pornographic content can be viewed on the Internet is damaging to children.

⇨ The above information is reprinted with kind permission from Premier Christian Media Trust and Safermedia, co-organisers of the Safetynet Campaign. Please visit www.safetynet.org.uk for further information.

© *Premier Christian Media Trust and Safermedia 2013*

*Note: the petition that Claire Perry took to Number 10 Downing street, referred to on page 7, was organised by Premier Christian Media Trust and Samermedia, co-organisers of the Safetynet Campaign.

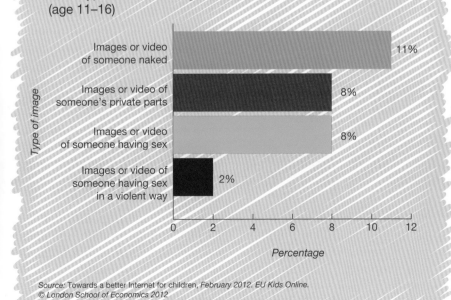

What type of sexual images have children seen on websites? (age 11–16)

Type of image	Percentage
Images or video of someone naked	11%
Images or video of someone's private parts	8%
Images or video of someone having sex	8%
Images or video of someone having sex in a violent way	2%

Percentage

Source: Towards a better Internet for children, *February 2012. EU Kids Online.*
© *London School of Economics 2012*

Should we panic about pornography?

The sexualisation threat could be over-hyped, says Alice Hoyle, but sexual bullying is still on the rise in schools. Education is the answer.

For years, concern has been increasing about the sexualisation of society and its negative effect on children and young people, but this perception may not be completely true. Research and evidence on the matter is insufficient and the views of young people have not been taken into account.

The definition of sexualisation seemingly incorporates everything from make-up and padded bras for girls aged eight and under to lads' mags, sexy music videos and erotic fiction. It even extends to hard-core pornography. Despite calls from children's charity the NSPCC to develop a tighter definition, consensus has still not been reached. The result is a moral panic about children and young people being sexualised by the media, but without a clear definition of what sexualisation actually is.

The Government has ordered two reviews of sexualisation in the past two years, but the latest version excluded sex and relationships education from its recommendations. And the Government is yet to update the Department for Education's Sex and Relationships Education Guidance, which is now 12 years out of date.

This education is vital for young people, who are developing as sexual beings. Avoiding the issue, or focusing only on the negatives, is not good enough.

Is it any wonder that teachers are reluctant to tackle such hot topics? They recognise the need to confront the issue but fear getting it wrong. One experienced PSHE teacher, who wishes to remain anonymous, says she was given some Internet safety resources by a local authority, with a bewildered admission that it 'did not know how to address other issues around porn'. Given the technological advances of recent years and the access pupils now have to pornographic materials, we cannot close our eyes to reality.

Schools are increasingly having to deal with cases of sexting (transmitting sexy images and messages via mobile phones and other devices). The young people involved have no idea that, even if they are under 18, this could be classed as making, using or distributing child pornography.

I know of one 14-year-old boy in care who searched the Internet for '14-year-olds having sex' because he wanted to see what his peers were up to. Unwittingly, this created huge safeguarding issues as he was effectively looking at child pornography.

Without guidance, young people who want to know more about sex may turn to pornography. But what effect is pornography having on them? Anecdotal concerns are that watching it encourages anal sex, the removal of pubic hair and even increased numbers of women seeking labiaplasty. Incidences of sexting, sexual harassment and sexual bullying in schools are increasingly being reported. A new report by ChildLine says the number of calls from teenagers upset by seeing adult images has increased by 34 per cent in the past year.

Justin Hancock, an award-winning sex educator and creator of the pornography education resource Planet Porn, says boys have told him they think women in pornography films are screaming because sex is hurting them. 'I have to explain that this is just bad acting and that sex should feel really pleasurable, not painful,' he says.

But we still need to talk about it. 'Porn education is not just about porn: it offers opportunities to explore self-esteem, body image, sexual decision-making, boundaries, pleasure, orgasm, communication and safer sex,'

Hancock adds. 'It covers sexual safety, the law, feminism, equality, lust and love, emotions and relationships. Then there are masculine norms, heteronormative scripts, sexuality and oppression.

'Talking about porn can be a great way to engage with young people around these very important sex and relationships education subject areas.'

Young people of both sexes have reported that pornography creates unreal expectations. 'Makes you want to try new things, take it up a notch,' said one boy in a survey of 14- and 15-year-olds in Rochdale.

'They (boys) get really sick ideas from watching it, and if you don't want to do it then they complain,' was one girl's perspective.

Yet evidence on the impact of sexualised media on young people is mixed. The EU Kids Online survey of 25,000 young people across Europe found that exposure to pornography – and the level of distress or harm caused by such exposure – was much less than anticipated.

Clare Bale, a registered general nurse and former public health principal for sexual health, who conducted her PhD research with young people, argues that research into the effect of sexualised media is inconclusive. She says we need to explore young people's engagement with the media rather than their exposure to it, while acknowledging and promoting their sexual agency. A study conducted by children's charity UNICEF in 2009 found that fear of

being judged or labelled a 'slag' or a 'slut' impacts directly on a girl's use of condoms and sexual health services.

The effect of 'pornification' or 'sexualisation' on young people's emerging sexuality may not yet be clear, but concerns about it highlight the need for sex education practitioners to develop sessions exploring sexual ethics.

Schools that cover pornography effectively do so because they are sufficiently experienced, competent and confident in covering the basics of sex and relationships education, as well as in creating a safe learning environment. They establish firm ground rules, such as no personal stories, instead discussing general situations without identifying anyone.

And while they may examine sexy advertising or sexual content in music videos, they would not show material classed as pornographic and aimed at those aged 18 or over. To do that would be illegal.

These schools also have strategies for answering difficult questions and are comfortable dealing with controversial issues that pupils may spontaneously allude to in lessons. Crucially, teachers need the support of their senior management team and school policy.

'Students tend to respond very positively as soon as they realise that you stand as much chance of learning about how to have good sex from porn as you do from learning how to rob a casino from

watching *Ocean's Eleven* or drive a car from watching *The Fast and the Furious*,' says Spencer Williams, an experienced teacher who leads sex and relationships education in his Scarborough school.

Teachers need to be mindful of the debates and evidence on the effects of exposure to pornography and sexualised culture, some of which is undoubtedly concerning. But we also need to recognise that young people need our guidance. We must be confident in our abilities to get the basics of sex and relationships education right before we embark on the more controversial aspects of the curriculum.

Even if schools do not feel able to cover pornography as a specific topic, they should ensure that they are providing sex and relationships education that meets the needs of young people and includes exploration of sexual ethics. To do otherwise is to do our adults of tomorrow a great disservice.

Alice Hoyle is a teacher and freelance sex and relationships education adviser. Email her at sexedukation@gmail.com or follow her on Twitter at @SexEdUKation.

4 September 2012

⇨ The above information is reprinted with kind permission from TES Editorial. Please visit www.tes.co.uk for further information.

Teaching children about sex: pornography lessons in schools, anyone?

Schools Minister Liz Truss has said there is nothing to prevent schools from adding porn education to lessons – but showing children porn won't educate them about sex.

By Susan Elkin

Do you want teachers to give your kids lessons about the evils of pornography?

Some children are already addicted. They swap hard-core images on their phones in the playground and they know, often better than their parents how to access it on computers.

A sobering study – led by Professor Andy Pippen, lecturer in social responsibility in Information Technology, at Plymouth University – published last month found that some users are as young as 11. They develop 'unrealistic expectations' of sex which lead to cases such as the one in June of a boy, aged 12 at the time, who raped a nine-year-old girl after watching pornography online.

There is undoubtedly a problem. ChildLine counsellors have confirmed an increase in calls from children upset by pornography and deputy children's commissioner, Sue Berelowitz asserts that Internet pornography is a factor in at least half the cases of gang-based sex attacks. And we're not talking about the odd photograph of a pretty young woman with shapely breasts such as teenage boys have always panted over.

Liz Truss, Schools Minister, has now pointed out that there is nothing to prevent schools from adding pornography education to sex and relationships work, if they wish – and, indeed if they teach sex and relationships at all. The latter is not compulsory in England although it is in other parts of the UK. The National Association of Headteachers has called for pornography awareness to be taught from age ten.

Now, I don't actually have a solution to this problem but I am absolutely certain that formally trying to teach children about the dangers of pornography will only make things worse.

You cannot teach children successfully about anything using theory only – witness the much derided condom on a banana lesson. It isn't a procedure you can learn theoretically. You need to see it and do it.

If you're going to alert children to the dangers of pornography you will have to show them some – thereby completely defeating the object. There will be some pupils to whom this will be new. What a good way of introducing them to it as well as encouraging the ones who've already discovered it. You wouldn't pass a joint round a classroom as a way of teaching children about the dangers of cannabis, would you? Well, the same principle applies.

In practice, of course, no teacher is likely to risk being accused of sharing porn with children, so mentions, if they get into lessons at all, will be unillustrated and therefore ineffective. And what happens if you try to tell children that there's this foul, horrible, corruptive stuff about sex which some sick people love and might try to share but which they – the nice kids in your classroom – must on no account look at in case it harms them? Well we all know the one about the forbidden fruit. I can think of no better way to ensure that large numbers of children, curiosity aroused, then seek some pornography out to see what the fuss is about.

As a secondary English teacher I would – always and without exception – do my best to answer any question honestly and without fuss. Asked what pornography was or what I thought about it I used to explain that it involved writing, paintings, drawings, photographs or films of men and women (in various combinations) touching each other or having sex and that much of it is rather nasty. In my view, sex should be something private and loving between two people, I'd tell them since they'd asked me. Then I'd move on and it was usually enough. With older groups, of course, there might be scope – if it's relevant to the rest of the work you're doing - to discuss, for example, why pupils think pornography is as widespread as it is, the morality of making it and whether or not it should be controlled by law.

I loathe the idea of children and young teenagers looking at some of the filth which is available on the Internet with a single click in the right place – and it isn't in the least difficult to find. I've just checked. Although I couldn't get it off my screen fast enough, I typed two words into Google, and instantly got hard-core film.

David Cameron is in favour of action to curb pornography. He wants new computers to be completely blockable by parents to protect their children. There is also a call to make pornography accessible by law only to over-18s with proper verification checks. Both are good ideas although tech-savvy youngsters will enjoy the challenge of hacking through the safeguards.

What is definitely not a good idea is deliberately drawing attention to pornography in lessons at school.

28 November 2012

⇨ The above article originally appeared in *The Independent*. Please visit www.independent.co.uk for further information.

Government rejects automatic porn filters

By Cara Acred

In May 2012, the Coalition Government launched a consultation to examine the case for an 'automatic' block on inappropriate online content such as pornography. The suggestion came amidst increasing pressure to increase the safety of children online. Between June and September 2012 over 3,500 individuals and organisations were consulted on their views about parental controls. However, by December 2012 David Cameron announced that the Government had decided against a system using automatic filters.

Who was consulted?

There were 3,059 responses to the coalition document. The largest proportion of respondents were classed as general 'members of the public' (69%), closely followed by parents (22%) and grandparents/other family members (3%).

What did the consultation ask?

The consultation asked respondents five types of questions:

⇨ Questions examining which controls respondents already use to help their children stay safe online, and which they find the most useful.

⇨ Questions examining the kind of Internet content that children have been exposed to, what they are worried by, what they need to be protected from and whose responsibility this is.

⇨ Questions examining responses to three different systems proposed to tackle child safety online.

⇨ Questions examining how children learn about online safety, what can be done – apart from education – to increase online safety.

⇨ Questions examining responses from businesses/organisations.

Key findings

⇨ 71% of respondents believe that parents have the main responsibility for keeping children safe online.

⇨ 41% said that their children had already been exposed to online pornography, and 23% indicated that their child had been bullied online.

⇨ In order to protect their children, 44% of respondents currently block particular kinds of content (e.g. sites promoting harmful behaviours or pornography).

⇨ 29% of respondents rely on education to protect against online risks.

⇨ Just 8% of respondents ensure that their PC is in a common area of the house.

⇨ Respondents believe that bullying is the online behaviour their children worry about the most (47%).

⇨ Parents said that they need the most help with protecting their children from pornography (42%), although 29% indicated that didn't need any help at all.

⇨ 45% of respondents believe that education about online safety and existing tools would make it easier to use parental controls.

⇨ School, Internet service providers (ISPs) and parents were highlighted as the most trusted sources of information regarding online safety.

⇨ 48% of respondents were aware that the four main ISPs – BT, TalkTalk, Virgin Media and Sky – have signed up to a code of practice which says they will:

⇨ Provide parental controls free of charge.

⇨ Provide all new customers with an enforced choice of whether or not to use parental controls.

⇨ Improve the communication of information to parents explaining the benefits of parental controls.

⇨ Align the information they provide to parents so it is all consistent.

⇨ 10% believed that the ISPs' code of practice should apply to all customers, not just new ones, while 42% believed the decision to use parental controls should not be an enforced choice.

Responses to the proposed filter systems

Option one: Harmful content (e.g. pornography) would automatically be blocked by your ISP. This would include devices such as smartphones, tablets, etc. If you wanted this content to become available, you could ask for filters to be removed.

⇨ 14% said yes to this system

⇨ 85% said no

⇨ 1% said they weren't sure

Option two: On setting up your Internet service, you would be asked some questions about what kind of content you would like available. This would include categories like 15-rated films, information about drugs, social networking sites and pornography).

⇨ 9% said yes

⇨ 83% said no

⇨ 8% said they weren't sure

Option three: This would combine opinions one and two. You would be asked the same questions as in opinion two, but some would be automatically ticked for you (e.g.

pornography). You would have the chance to un-tick these options but failure to do so would cause that content to be blocked.

⇨ 7% said yes

⇨ 87% said no

⇨ 6% said they weren't sure

Conclusions

The Government chose not to pursue any of the proposed filtering systems proposed in the consultation because, on average, 85% of respondents rejected the use of any of proposed filter systems. The most popular reasons for disagreeing with the proposed options were:

⇨ Fear of blocking useful sites, such as Sexual Health websites, and the potential damage to small businesses.

⇨ Worry that automatic filters would create a false sense of security and lead people to become less cautious.

⇨ Taking responsibility away from parents.

The Government's response to the consultation findings notes that: 'The Internet provides children

and young people with a wealth of opportunities for their entertainment, communication, education and enrichment. But there are also risks of harm through the deliberate online behaviour of others, and through exposure to age-inappropriate content. As children live their lives in an increasingly digital world, they need to be as aware of the risks they face in the online world as in the offline world.' Their response emphasises that parents must take responsibility for keeping their children safe online and would like ISPs to 'encourage' parents to switch on filters.

Future action

The Government's future proposals include:

⇨ Working with ISPs to implement a new approach to parental controls.

⇨ Working with all businesses, information and communication industries to develop family-friendly Internet access.

⇨ Working with UKCCIS to:

⇨ Reach a solid definition of inappropriate online content.

⇨ Improve methods of identifying inappropriate content.

⇨ Establish clear classifications for parental controls.

⇨ Research the reasons why parental controls are not used by more parents.

⇨ Investigate more effective age-verification techniques.

Source: The Government's response to the consultation on parental Internet controls, *December 2012. Department of Education, 2012.*

Visit www.education.gov.uk to read the report in full.

⇨ The above article was written by Cara Acred on behalf of Independence Educational Publishers.

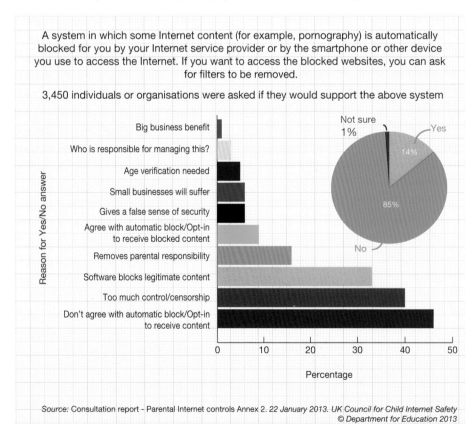

A system in which some Internet content (for example, pornography) is automatically blocked for you by your Internet service provider or by the smartphone or other device you use to access the Internet. If you want to access the blocked websites, you can ask for filters to be removed.

3,450 individuals or organisations were asked if they would support the above system

Source: Consultation report - Parental Internet controls Annex 2. *22 January 2013.* UK Council for Child Internet Safety
© Department for Education 2013

What is prostitution?

Information from Politics.co.uk.

Prostitution describes the offering and provision of sexual services for financial gain.

In the UK, prostitution itself is not illegal but there are a number of offences linked to it. For example, it is an offence to control a prostitute for gain, or to keep a brothel.

Prostitution has a close affinity with a host of other important social issues, in particular crime, drugs, sexual equality, poverty and health.

Although there are exceptions, most prostitutes are women selling their services to men.

Background

Prostitution is sometimes referred to as 'the oldest profession', as it meets the natural urges of humans in return for money, and is often claimed to be as old as civilisation itself.

The legal regulation of prostitution in the UK was set out in the Sexual Offences Act 1956, which reflected the findings of the Wolfenden Committee investigation into prostitution and homosexuality that took place around that time.

The Wolfenden Committee treated prostitution and its status in the law as a moral issue and this was reflected in the text of the Act. This led to famous debates between Lord Devlin and the philosopher Herbert Hart.

In late 2003 the Home Office announced its intention to review the laws on prostitution with the aim of overhauling the dated regulations of the 1956 Act. Subsequently amendments relating to prostitution were made under the Sexual Offences Act 2003 with regard to the following offences; 'causing or inciting prostitution for gain', 'controlling prostitution for gain', 'penalties for keeping a brothel used for prostitution' and 'extension of gender specific prostitution offences'.

The Policing and Crime Bill, introduced to the Commons in December 2008, created a new offence of paying for sex with someone who is controlled for gain and introduced new powers to close brothels; it also modified the law on soliciting. The Bill received Royal Assent in November 2009.

Controversies

As with all matters of sexuality, prostitution continues to be debated on both social and moral levels. Opponents of prostitution and moral conservatives believe the practice is intrinsically morally corrupt and a challenge to family values, therefore regarding a ban to be justified in the name of public morality. Many religious groups adopt this position, adding another aspect to the debate.

However, many who regard involvement in prostitution as a matter of private morality still argue for legal regulation.

Prostitution's quasi-criminal status has led it to be closely associated with organised crime, poverty, drugs, child abuse and people trafficking.

Virtual imprisonment has become a particular problem in recent years, notably since the fall of the Iron Curtain and the break-up of Yugoslavia. There has been an increase in the 'white slave trade' from Eastern Europe and Russia, along with a general influx of organised crime, with many women thought to be living as virtual slaves.

Because prostitutes have large numbers of sexual partners, they are more likely to have sexually transmitted infections and be vectors for spreading these infections – adding a public health dimension to the debate.

The previous Labour Government said it wanted to reduce prostitution in the UK and, as some said legal controls were too blunt a tool, tried to establish what policies would work. For example, in 2002 the Government made a total of £850,000 available for groups working in a multi-agency context to implement local strategies for reducing prostitution-related crime and disorder.

Some argue that licensed brothels would help to ensure worker safety, keep them off the streets, help prevent health problems, bring revenue to the Treasury and remove the need for exploitative and abusive pimps. However, many others find this morally repugnant.

The murders of five prostitutes in Ipswich in November and December 2006 reignited calls for a new approach to tackling the issue.

In November 2008 the Home Office published the findings of a six-month review into how the demand for prostitution could be reduced. Home Secretary Jacqui Smith, in a foreword to the review, stated: 'So far, little attention has been focused on the sex buyer, the person responsible for creating the demand for prostitution markets. And it is time for that to change.'

But Government plans to create a new law under the Policing and Crime Bill making it an offence to pay for sex with someone who is 'controlled by another for gain' caused particular controversy. Even if the person paying for sex was unaware that the prostitute was trafficked or controlled by a pimp, they would still be liable for prosecution and if convicted would be given a criminal record and a fine of up to £1,000.

The Bar Council warned that the offence as drafted risked convictions that may be seen as unfair by reasonable people and that such convictions would bring the criminal law into disrepute, particularly given the stigma that would result.

Concerns were also raised by several MPs including the Labour chair of the Home Affairs Select Committee, Keith Vaz, who said that he was 'not convinced that the best course of action is to prosecute in the proposed way men who go into situations where they wish to buy sex from prostitutes'.

And Shadow Justice Minister, Henry Bellingham stated, 'We do not in any way want to stand up for the people who feel they have to, in unfortunate circumstances, go and use prostitutes. We are concerned, however, about bringing in credible law that will stand the test of being put through the courts.'

The Coalition Government was strongly criticised in the Spring of 2010 for declining to support a proposal for an EU directive to prevent and combat trafficking in human beings and to protect the victims who were trafficked for different purposes, including into the sex industry.

The Government did, however, promise to review its decision when the finalised text was agreed and in March 2011, having scrutinised the final text, announced that it would now apply to opt-in to the new EU directive (2011/36/EU) on trafficking in human beings.

In December 2011, the Home Office launched a national 'Ugly Mugs' pilot scheme to help protect sex workers from violent and abusive individuals. The Home Office is providing £108,000 to fund the 12-month pilot which includes establishing a national online network to bring together and support locally run 'Ugly Mug' schemes.

These local 'Ugly Mug'/dodgy punter schemes have been running for some years and, according to the UK Network of Sex Work Projects, have proved very useful in passing on warnings to sex workers about dangerous people, as well as helping to increase the reporting, detection and conviction of crimes.

The pilot scheme is being run by the UKNSWP.

In March 2012, the Greater London Authority published a report on the policing of off-street sex work and sex trafficking in London. Entitled *Silence on Violence – Improving the Safety of Women*, the report was written by Assembly Member Andrew Boff at the request of the London Mayor following a number of questions raised during Mayor's Question Time.

Mr Boff found evidence that sex workers were reporting fewer crimes to police and that raids had increased in some parts of London. He made a number of recommendations including involving sex workers in police strategies that involve them and prioritising crime against sex workers by labelling it as a hate crime.

Statistics

The Sexual Offences Act 2003 creates three offences of trafficking for the purposes of sexual exploitation: Section 57 for trafficking into the UK; Section 58 for trafficking within the UK; and Section 59 for trafficking out of the UK.

Section 46(1) of the Criminal Justice and Police Act 2001 creates an offence to place advertisements relating to prostitution on, or in the immediate vicinity of, a public telephone an advertisement relating to prostitution.

Children under 18 involved in prostitution should be treated as victims of abuse. Those who use child prostitutes should be prosecuted under Sections 47 and 51 of the Sexual Offences Act 2003.

Section 16 of the Policing and Crime Act 2009 amends section 1(1) of the Street Offences Act 1959 to create an offence for a person (whether male or female) persistently to loiter or solicit in a street or public place for the purposes of offering services as a prostitute. This is with effect from 1 April 2010.

The term 'common prostitute' has now been removed.

Section 1(4) has been amended to insert that for the purposes of section 1, conduct is persistent if it takes place on two or more occasions in any period of three months.

HOLD ON A SECOND LUV, JUST RUNNING A QUICK CHECK ON YOU.

Section 1(5) provides that in deciding whether a person's conduct is persistent, any conduct that took place before the commencement of this section will be disregarded.

Section 19 of the Policing and Crime Act 2009 introduces section 51A into the Sexual Offences Act 2003 and creates a new offence for a person in a street or public place to solicit another for the purpose of obtaining a sexual service as a prostitute. The reference to a person in a street or public place includes a person in a motor vehicle in a street or public place.

This replaces the offences of kerb crawling and persistent soliciting under sections 1 and 2 of the Sexual Offences Act 1985 with effect from 1 April 2010.

A person guilty of an offence under this section is liable on summary conviction to a fine not exceeding level 3 on the standard scale.

Source: The Crown Prosecution Service.

Quotes

'The Government's ambition is to end all forms of violence against women and girls. This includes protecting those involved in prostitution, who are particularly vulnerable to violent and sexual crimes.

'"Ugly Mugs" schemes encourage individuals to report incidents so that others can be safeguarded in the future, and more perpetrators can be brought to justice.

'Local agencies are best placed to find solutions to local problems but where schemes are effective in protecting individuals and communities we want to share information and best practice.'

Home Office Minister, Lynne Featherstone, launching the 'Ugly Mugs' pilot scheme – December 2011.

'There is a group in London who are at least 12 times more likely to be murdered than the national average.

Approximately three quarters of those within this category will also be subjected to violence, assault and rape.

'However, this group often distrusts the police and are much less willing to report crimes against them than the national average.

'The group referred to are sex workers and it is imperative that we improve their safety in London.'

Andrew Boff, leader of the Conservative group in the London Assembly – 2012.

⇨ The above information is reprinted with kind permission from Politics.co.uk. Please visit www.politics.co.uk for further information.

Prostitution – the facts

The oldest profession – or the oldest oppression? The facts on prostitution speak for themselves.

'Hell de Jour'

⇨ 75% of women involved in prostitution started as children.

⇨ 74% of women cite poverty as the primary motivator for entering prostitution (Melrose 2002).

⇨ Up to 70% of women in prostitution spent time in care, 45% report sexual abuse and 85% physical abuse within their families (Home Office 2006).

⇨ Up to 95% of women in prostitution are problematic drug users, including around 78% heroin users and rising numbers of crack cocaine addicts (Home Office 2004a).

⇨ More than half of UK women in prostitution have been raped and/or seriously sexually assaulted. At least three quarters have been physically assaulted (Home Office 2004b).

⇨ 68% of women in prostitution meet the criteria for Post Traumatic Stress Disorder in the same range as torture victims and combat veterans undergoing treatment (Ramsey et al. 1993).

⇨ Four out of five women working in London brothels are thought to be foreign nationals (Dickson 2004).

⇨ The mortality rate women in prostitution in London suffer is 12 times the national average (Home Office 2004a).

⇨ A global study of prostitution found that nine out of ten women in prostitution would like to exit if they could (Farley, 2003).

⇨ Ten years ago it was estimated that around 80,000 women were in prostitution in the UK (Kinnell 1999). Many experts believe the number to be far higher now.

The effects on wider society

The prostitution industry also harms women in wider society.

Normalising prostitution normalises an extreme form of sexual subordination and objectification; it legitimises the existence of an underclass of women and it reinforces male dominance over women.

It also undermines our struggle for gender equality as it undermines efforts to combat sexual harassment and male violence in the home, the workplace and the streets if men can buy the right to perpetrate these very same acts against women and girls in prostitution.

"Treating prostitution like any other job doesn't deal with the long-term psychological and physical effects of having unwanted and often violent sex"

Solutions

So, what do we do about this oldest oppression?

Criminalise demand

The last thing we want is for people in prostitution to be criminalised. We therefore call for decriminalisation for all prostituted people (who are mainly women and children) and the criminalisation of all people who use prostituted people.

This approach has been adopted by Nordic countries such as Sweden, Norway and Iceland – nations which consistently top the global polls in terms of gender equality.

The 'Nordic model' completely decriminalises those who sell sex acts whilst offering support services to exit prostitution. It further criminalises the purchase of sex acts to tackle the demand which expands prostitution and fuels trafficking for sexual exploitation.

This sends out a powerful message that it is not acceptable for women's bodies to be bought and sold like commodities for sexual use and it overturns outdated legislation which essentially enshrines men's right to buy women by focussing on those who sell sex acts whilst ignoring those who buy them.

In this way, the 'Nordic model' shifts criminal liability away from those who are exploited through prostitution and towards those who contribute to this exploitation by choosing to buy sex acts.

Furthermore, the 'Nordic' model has a broad and progressive political vision in that it actually aims to end the exploitative industry of prostitution rather than legitimise it which essentially ends up expanding it.

Why decriminalisation does not work

Total decriminalisation of the whole industry – including of pimps, traffickers and punters – does not make women safer. Why?

As the market for prostitution expands, so does the illegal sector. In New Zealand, where the entire industry has been legalised – the illegal sector has actually expanded more than the legal sector. The illegal sector now makes up 80% of the industry (Instone and Margerison 2007).

This has also happened in Amsterdam where authorities have made a U-turn on legalisation and are now closing down areas of the red light district. According to the Mayor of Amsterdam 'it is impossible to create a safe and controllable zone for women that is not open to abuse by organised crime' (Bindel and Kelly 2004).

Furthermore, decriminalisation of the entire industry and treating prostitution like any other job doesn't deal with the long-term psychological and physical effects of having unwanted and often violent and abusive sex numerous times a day and having to act like you enjoy it and are turned on by it.

Jo, a former prostituted woman who started at the age of 13 says:

'When was the last time you enjoyed being penetrated by 20 lairy, half-pissed blokes who spit all over you, call you a variety

of names and demand you act as though you are really getting off on it in an evening, every evening?'

To be able to do this many women need to 'split off' from this process in their head, hence why drug and alcohol dependency is such a big part of prostitution.

To make women in prostitution safer we have to offer exit strategies and support to get out of prostitution, not legitimise commercial sexual exploitation by making it legal and by giving a green light for the industry to expand.

Furthermore, we have to work towards ending the exploitative industry of prostitution to ensure that future generations of vulnerable women and children are no longer drawn into or coerced into having to sell their bodies. To do this we have to tackle the problem at its root – we have to tackle demand.

⇨ The above information is reprinted with kind permission from Object. Please visit www.object.org.uk for further information.

Know your rights: An A – Z for sex workers

From the English Collective of Prostitutes, The 'Girls' Union'.

We are a network of women who work or have worked in different areas of the sex industry – both on the streets and indoors.

Since 1975, we have been campaigning for decriminalisation and safety of sex workers. We help sex workers defend themselves against criminal charges and have won precedent legal cases like the first private prosecution for rape in England which put a serial rapist behind bars. We fight against having a criminal record which prevents us getting other jobs. And we fight for housing, higher benefits and wages so that any of us can leave prostitution if and when we want.

If you need our support or want to support our work please get in touch. You can also help by donating: by cheque or through our website. The prostitution laws are so unjust and devious that it is essential that sex workers, no matter where we work, know the law, how to protect ourselves from arrest, how to defend ourselves if charged and where to get help. The public also need to know about the laws which are passed in their name. Putting together our experience as sex workers with the experience of community workers and legal professionals, we can prevent the law from being misused against us at the same time as we campaign to get the laws abolished.

This rights sheet was researched and written with help from many working girls, male sex workers and others.

We can't list all the names as so many of us have to remain anonymous until the laws are abolished.

Loitering and soliciting

What happens if the police stop you in the street?

The police can stop anyone under suspicion of 'loitering or soliciting in a street or public place for the purposes of offering services as a prostitute'. They may try to search you. Try to stop them. A search is only legal if they suspect that you are likely to commit an offence or are carrying a weapon.

The label 'common prostitute' has been abolished but prostitute cautions continue. You have to be cautioned twice, on two separate occasions, before you can be charged for the first time. The cautions are recorded at the police station and you don't have to admit guilt to get one.

If you are arrested ask to see evidence of the caution/s. Be sure to ask for the dates. If the police can't show proof of your cautions, they'll have to drop the charges. The right to appeal a caution has been abolished.

If you are convicted of soliciting you can be forced to agree to an 'Engagement and Support Order' or the court may try to persuade you saying it is an alternative to a fine.

This order means you have to attend three meetings with a supervisor (usually a probation officer or a project outreach worker) to address the 'causes of your offending'. There is no requirement for the supervisor to provide help with benefits, income, housing, debt or anything practical. Many sex workers object to this waste of their time. If you breach the order, you can be arrested, held for 72 hours, brought back to court and fined.

The maximum fine for loitering and soliciting is £500 for a first offence and £1,000 for a second offence. The offence should be taken off your record after a year.

ASBO – Anti-Social Behaviour Orders

These civil orders are issued for allegedly causing 'harassment, alarm or distress to one or more persons'. The first penalty is a ban from a particular area or from a particular kind of activity but if you breach the order you commit a criminal offence and can be sentenced to up to five years in prison. Hearsay evidence is allowed. That is no witnesses come to court to give evidence, only police officers who claim to be reporting on what they were told by anonymous people. Such 'evidence' is often inaccurate, exaggerated and even fabricated. You can get legal aid to challenge ASBOs.

The caution system doesn't apply to Scotland.

Brothel keeping, massage parlours, saunas

What is a brothel?

Two or more prostitutes living together or sharing premises for work constitutes a brothel. You don't have to be there at the same time, it is still a brothel if two or more women work on different days. Brothel-keeping prosecutions are increasing so it is crucial that you know your rights.

Don't let the police in without a warrant and don't give a statement. The police have to show that the place is a brothel – that more than one woman is working there. They also need evidence of sexual activity and to show that whoever they accuse of running the brothel knew sex was being offered. If they find work rotas, menus of sexual services, etc., this can be used as evidence against you. If the premises or the bills are in your name, or they find evidence that you pay other girls, you are more likely to be prosecuted and found guilty. The police can take any computers and your phone if you are arrested.

Some women have been found not guilty by showing that the flat was run in a collective way with no one woman being overall in charge. Some women have brought evidence to court to show they had to work with other women for safety.

What to do if there is a raid

The police cannot come in without a warrant so don't let them in. Write down the name and number of all the officers. Insist on being present in every room they search. Do not let them take photographs or film footage of you. Insist on a receipt for all monies and other items taken. Take your own pictures as they open any safe to find any money. It is common for money to disappear during a raid.

If you are arrested you'll be taken to the police station for questioning – don't panic. Ask for a lawyer immediately. Say as little as possible. You may be kept overnight (or up to 48 hours).

Can a landlord let premises to a prostitute?

Yes, to one prostitute alone. But s/he can't let the premises knowing that they'll be used as a brothel (more than one sex worker). Selling sex may be a breach of your tenancy agreement (many have bans on 'illegal' or 'immoral' use). But you can't be evicted overnight – the landlord will have to take you to court. It is illegal for a tenant to allow their flat etc. to be used for habitual prostitution (even by one sex worker).

The maximum fine for brothel-keeping is six months in prison if the case is heard in a magistrates court and seven years in prison if heard in the crown court.

Closure orders

What powers do the police and courts have to close down premises?

The police or local authority can slap a closure notice on the door of a flat or house if they suspect that the premises are being used for 'specified prostitution or pornography offences'. Then they must apply to the court within 48 hours for a closure order. Anyone who lives there or who has an interest in the premises can oppose the order.

Women have won against closure orders by challenging police evidence which is nearly always hearsay (no witnesses come to court, the police just reported what they 'had been told') and is often inaccurate, exaggerated or even fabricated. The orders last for three months.

Causing, inciting and controlling prostitution for gain

What counts as 'controlling a prostitute'?

This offence is quite wide. Not only is it used against managers it has also been used against women working together who have been charged with controlling each other. The police have to show that you organised someone's work and got money for it, so renting premises, organising a work rota, paying bills, hiring and firing can count as evidence. No evidence of force is needed to get a conviction.

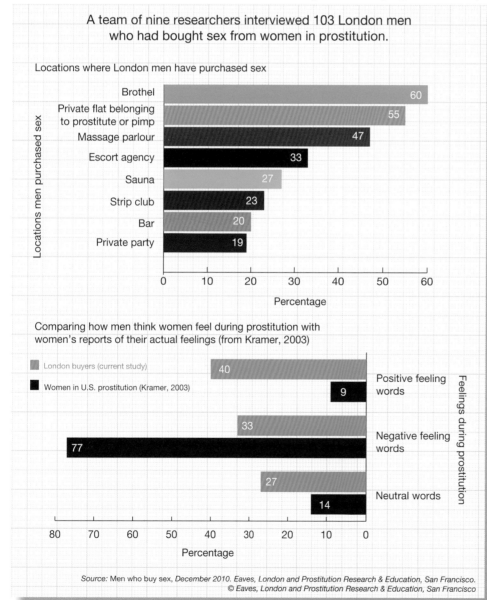

A team of nine researchers interviewed 103 London men who had bought sex from women in prostitution.

Locations where London men have purchased sex

Locations men purchased sex:
- Brothel: 60
- Private flat belonging to prostitute or pimp: 55
- Massage parlour: 47
- Escort agency: 33
- Sauna: 27
- Strip club: 23
- Bar: 20
- Private party: 19

Percentage (0–60)

Comparing how men think women feel during prostitution with women's reports of their actual feelings (from Kramer, 2003)

- London buyers (current study)
- Women in U.S. prostitution (Kramer, 2003)

Feelings during prostitution:
- Positive feeling words: London buyers 40, Women in U.S. prostitution 9
- Negative feeling words: London buyers 33, Women in U.S. prostitution 77
- Neutral words: London buyers 27, Women in U.S. prostitution 14

Percentage (80–0)

Source: Men who buy sex, December 2010. Eaves, London and Prostitution Research & Education, San Francisco.
© Eaves, London and Prostitution Research & Education, San Francisco

The sentence can vary from probation to seven years depending on the seriousness.

Causing or Inciting is used against anyone who encourages someone (over the age of 18) into prostitution or makes the practice of prostitution easier.

Escort agencies and night clubs

How do agencies and clubs get closed down for prostitution?

Bosses of agencies providing outcalls could get busted for controlling if the police show that women are providing sexual services with the knowledge of the management.

Doing business in hotels

What do you do if you are stopped by the security?

If you are visiting a client, phone the client through the house phone and ask him to come down for you. If security ask you into another room refuse to go. The only power they have is to ask you to leave. If you are resident at the hotel and they accuse you of prostitution ask why. You are allowed to have guests.

Lapdancing/stripping

Strip clubs are now classified as 'sexual entertainment venues', the cost of licenses has increased and local authorities have been given greater powers to control the number of clubs in a particular area or ban them altogether. Dancers are protesting against the closures of clubs and the increased monitoring and regulation of dancers by management.

Trafficking

The laws that are supposed to protect victims of trafficking are often used to deport immigrant sex workers and to justify raids on flats where no-one is being trafficked or coerced.

Most people understand trafficking as bringing people into the country by force or deception, coercing them to work and keeping them captive by threats and violence. But the law on trafficking for sexual exploitation in the UK (unlike most other countries) criminalises anyone who helps a person to come to, leave or move around the UK, if she then ends up working in the sex industry, regardless of whether there is any force, threats or coercion. Immigrant sex workers have been convicted for giving another sex worker a lift from the airport.

Some women who have been held captive and forced to have sex for money have escaped with the help of sex workers. They have learned some English and got help to stash away some money so when they were ready to escape they could survive without going to the authorities who they feared would deport them. Laws against trafficking (like laws on soliciting, controlling and brothel-keeping) discourage sex workers from working together and helping each other.

Even though under trafficking law the police don't have to show that anyone was forced or coerced, guidelines for prosecutors do state that trafficking is only present if the victim is being forced, so anything that shows a non-coercive relationship between you and anyone you are accused of trafficking is helpful to your defence.

Advertising

Is it legal to advertise?

No. It's against the law to advertise sexual services on the web, in shop windows, newspapers, contact magazines, etc. Some sex workers do advertise using 'escort', 'model', etc. You can advertise in this way and work legally from your place as long as you are alone. Putting cards in phone boxes is illegal.

Proceeds of crime law

This law is being used a lot against sex workers. It seems to be a primary reason that prosecutions have increased. It is used to seize savings, assets (like your house, car, jewellery) and demand payment of any income you have made as a result of what they judge to be criminal activity.

What is particularly unfair is that the burden of proof is reversed so you have to prove that your money did not come from criminal activity.

It is proceeds of a crime not profit of a crime so if you made £200 a week and spent £50 a week on expenses you owe £200. Confiscation orders can extend to family, partners and jointly owned businesses and investigators can go back six years.

You usually get six months to pay and if you don't pay you can face imprisonment. Unlike other fines, when you come out of prison you will still have to pay to amount of the order.

You don't have to use the same lawyer for POCA as you did for the criminal case.

Clients

Is asking a woman for sex on the street legal?

No. Clients soliciting for sex and kerb-crawling can be arrested on their first offence and the police don't have to show that they caused a nuisance. If convicted they may be offered a 'rehabilitation' course (John's school) or fined up to £1,000. They can also be disqualified from driving or have their car confiscated.

A new offence of 'paying for sex with a prostitute subject to force and coercion' was introduced in 2010. The client can get convicted whether or not he knew the sex worker was being forced, and regardless of what efforts he made to find out. In court, the police have to show that the sex worker was coerced or exploited. The maximum sentence is six months or a fine of £1,000.

⇨ The above information is reprinted with kind permission from the English Collective of Prostitutes. Please visit www.prostitutecollective.net for further information.

© English Collective of Prostitutes 2013

Men who buy sex

Who they buy and what they know.

This report has included details of the often significant knowledge held by buyers about women in prostitution, and their frank discussions of their experiences buying sex. Following are some highlights of findings from this report.

1. 55% of 103 London men who bought sex believed that a majority of people in prostitution were lured, tricked or trafficked.

Information and explanation of the newly introduced legislation on demand, which makes it an offence to purchase sex from someone who has been subjected to exploitation (Policing and Crime Act, 2009), should be part of public awareness campaigns aimed at reducing or eliminating men's demand for prostitution. The law and the potential consequences of paying for sex need to be explained to current and potential buyers. In addition, general public awareness of men's knowledge about trafficking and coercion in the sex industry is important.

2. Today, prostitution has moved indoors; 96% of these men used women in indoor prostitution (brothels, flats, saunas, massage parlours).

Based on these 103 London men's reports of coercive control, pimping and trafficking, it can no longer be assumed that indoor prostitution is safer than street prostitution. On the contrary, it appears that many of the most vulnerable women are kept under control indoors, not in the street where they would be seen by the public or by police.

Local and national newspapers cannot justify selling advertising space to brothel owners and organisers of indoor prostitution. A blanket ban on advertising of this nature should be introduced.

3. More than half of the interviewees confirmed they were in a relationship at the time they used women in prostitution.

This contradicts the common misperception that men buy sex because they are lonely or have no partners.

The disappointment expressed by men seeking the 'girlfriend experience' in prostitution should be highlighted in any awareness campaign. There are men who are sold the idea that 'buying' a partner is possible and that prostituted women can fulfil that role.

4. Many of the men felt that at various times during prostitution, women had no rights at all.

Attitudes normalising rape were common among this group of men who buy sex in London. Over half of the interviewees believed that men would 'need' to rape if they did not have access to prostituted women.

There is no evidence supporting the theory that prostitution prevents rape. Experts in rape and other forms of sexual violence must ensure that myths that prostitution prevents rape are debunked.

5. For 29% of the men, prostitution was their first sexual experience.

The youngest interviewee was 18 years of age, confirming the need for public education programmes aimed at boys. Personal, Social, Health and Economic Education (PSHE) sessions should contain content to deter young men from becoming buyers. More than 40% of the men interviewed in this study were accompanied by friends or family the first time they bought sex. Peer pressure was a significant 'pull factor' for many of the men interviewed for this study. Public awareness campaigns could play an important role in primary prevention of prostitution. The ambivalence about buying sex expressed by many interviewees could be highlighted in such a campaign.

6. Legalisation and prostitution tolerance zones encouraged men to buy sex. Several men explained that once having visited areas where prostitution is legal or

promoted, they returned to the UK with a renewed dedication to buying sex even if that practice is illegal.

The new UK legislation needs to be enforced extra-territorially. Almost half of the men had paid for sex in other countries, mostly in legalised regimes such as The Netherlands.

7. Many men stated that pornography informed their decisions to request specific acts with women in prostitution and also with non-prostituting sex partners. Other interviewees stated that pornography use led to their paying for sex.

Further research into the connections between pornography and prostitution, particularly in relation to attitudes towards women and sexual violence, needs to be conducted in the UK.

8. One-fifth of the men had paid for sex while serving in the Armed Forces.

UK policy and deterrents like those adopted by the United Nations during the Balkan crisis are advisable.

9. In England, Scotland and the US, men agreed that being placed on a sex offender register would most effectively deter them from buying sex. They also agreed that other deterrents such as prison time or public exposure would be effective.

The least effective deterrent, according to interviewees in Scotland, the US and London would be an educational programme without the threat of prison. An educational programme for sex buyers would be well advised to operate in conjunction with the Criminal Justice System and never as a substitute for criminal sanctions.

More than three-quarters of interviewees acknowledged that greater criminal penalties would deter them from paying for sex, and yet only 6% had ever been arrested for soliciting prostitution. New and existing legislation needs to be vigorously implemented. A public awareness campaign to accompany enforcement of laws against buying sex might be modelled on the 2006 anti-smoking campaign.

10. Of 103 London men who had bought sex, two-thirds said that being issued an ASBO would be a deterrent.

Currently in London, ASBOs are routinely issued to women in street prostitution but rarely to men apprehended as kerb crawlers. Such measures need to be used against buyers.

11. 65% of interviewees believed that 'most men pay for sex'.

General public education and awareness campaigns are essential in challenging men's demand for

WHY DO MEN BUY SEX?

1 Satisfy immediate sexual urge, entertainment, pleasure: 32%

2 Seeks variety, wants to select certain physical, racial and sexual stereotypes: 21%

3 Can't get what he wants sexually or emotionally in his current relationship: 20%

4 Convenience, no commitment, no emotional connection: 15%

5 It's a thrill; likes to break a taboo: 8%

6 It's an addiction or compulsion or result of intoxication: 3%

7 Male bonding, peer pressure: 2%

* Primary reasons for buying sex, according to 103 London men – multiple responses possible.

prostitution. An approach to public education about prostitution would be to emphasise the marginalised status of men who buy sex rather than viewing their activity as part of the mainstream.

12. Most men (71%) said they felt ambivalence about paying for sex. They often felt guilt or shame about buying sex while at the same time continuing to use prostituted women, hiding those behaviours.

The men avoided emotional involvement with women in prostitution while at the same time seeking the appearance of a relationship. Lacking accurate empathy with the objects of their sexual purchase, the men were usually unable to determine what the women actually thought or felt, including the women's lack of genuine sexual interest.

Men's ambivalence about prostitution might serve as a point of entry to educational programmes that promote sustained deterrence from buying sex.

Some men said they were unable to imagine a world in which prostitution could ever be ended. When asked what they thought might bring about an end to the sex trade, responses such as, 'kill every girl in the world', and 'you'd need to put all men in solitary cells' highlighted the fact that for many, prostitution is viewed as an inevitability. Others could see possibilities for change. 'The challenge,' said one interviewee, 'is to change the way men think.'

Men's attitudes play a central role in perpetrating violence against women. Efforts to prevent violence against women must address not only those attitudes which are overtly condoning of violence against women, but also the wider clusters of attitudes related to sex, including prostitution, which normalise and justify this violence (Flood and Pease, 2009).

A majority of these men were aware of specific instances of trafficking for prostitution. Often, they knew that they were using trafficked women for sex. Trafficking is associated with brothel and massage parlour prostitution in the UK. Trafficking victims from Brazil, Lithuania and

Thailand were discovered at a 2009 Reading brothel raid (Roberts, 2009). Traffickers have the capacity to hide human trafficking in the huge volume of travel facilitated by globalisation. They can also neutralise or overcome regulatory measures imposed by governments through corruption and co-option (Williams, 2009). Organised criminals who traffic women to London for prostitution have the capacity to rapidly modify trafficking operations to reflect changing risks, to forge high-quality documents; to use front companies; to use advanced technology such as satellite phones, GPS, and digital surveillance; to use defence lawyers who are skilled at defending organised criminals; and to launder funds from trafficking via sophisticated methods (Picarelli, 2009).

Specifically referring to the goal of ending sex trafficking, in late 2009, United Nations Secretary-General Ban Ki-moon called for greater efforts to tackle the global pandemic of violence against women and girls, emphasising that the international community must demand accountability and take concrete steps to end impunity (UN News Centre, 2009). Since it is known that prostitution is associated with extremely high levels of violence against women (Watts and Zimmerman, 2002), and based on this study it is known that many of the men who buy prostituted women are aware of the crimes of pimping, coercive control, lack of opportunity for escape and trafficking, the next logical step would be to move forward with stronger legal and social deterrents for the sex buyer.

⇨ The above information is reprinted with kind permission from Eaves, London and Prostitution Research & Education, San Francisco. Please visit www.combattrafficking.eu for further information.

Prostitute Rita Brown calls for legalised brothels in Stoke-on-Trent

Working girl Rita Brown wrote to Prime Minister David Cameron from her prison cell – to ask for prostitution to be decriminalised.

The 60-year-old, who went by the name 'Crystal', was sentenced to eight months in jail after she admitted running a brothel since 1996.

Now, after being released from HMP Foston Hall prison, she has revealed how she rubbed shoulders with killers during her time behind bars, and campaigned vigorously for prostitution to be regulated.

And Ms Brown, who plans to go back into the sex trade, told how she penned a letter to Downing Street, calling on the PM to listen to her pleas.

The masseur is also calling for Staffordshire Police and Stoke-on-Trent City Council managers to meet sex workers to discuss ways to better manage prostitution across Stoke-on-Trent.

She believes prostitutes should be required to pay a £50 annual registration fee in return for legal protection.

The 60-year-old, of Seabridge Lane, Newcastle, said: 'There are about 600 prostitutes in Stoke-on-Trent, so that would be £30,000 to the council every year.

'The girls would have to register where they were working and it would be safer. Girls who stole, or who broke the rules, could have their licence taken away. It would protect the girls and the clients.'

Ms Brown broke down in tears as she was jailed in September, after she admitted keeping a brothel for prostitution between 1 July 1996 and 6 February last year.

However, she maintains she never acted as a brothel 'madam', and shared accommodation at the Caress massage parlour in Middleport with other girls for 'safety'.

She says she made her own living as a prostitute.

'Not one part of me wanted to plead guilty, but I was told if I didn't I would be found guilty, and then I would get a longer sentence,' she said.

'I cried every night for six weeks. I couldn't eat or sleep.

'Other prisoners told me I couldn't cry because it was pathetic.

'It was horrendous. I wanted to kill myself, but there is no way of killing yourself in prison.

'You are locked up from 8.15pm to 8.15am during the week, and from 5.15pm at weekends. There is no access to toilets.

'I suffered from verbal bullying.

The younger ones said some really cruel things and would try to trip me up.

'The ones who had done some really nasty crimes, the killers, were some of the kindest people in there.'

Chief Inspector Adrian Roberts, commander of the Stoke-on-Trent North Local Policing Team, spelt out the police's position on prostitution.

He said: 'Prostitution is against the law, and whatever the political or moral viewpoints people want to have, as police officers it is our job to uphold the law.

'Prostitution is an unlawful activity and if we become aware it is going on, we will take action. We are not going to turn a blind eye to the concerns of the community.'

A spokeswoman for working girls charity, the English Collective of Prostitutes, said: 'What a terrible injustice that Rita Brown was imprisoned for working together with other women for safety.

'Ms Brown's case and her campaign to win a change in police and council policy must be the impetus for change, so no other woman's life is destroyed by imprisonment and a criminal record.'

A spokesman for 10 Downing Street said a reply to Ms Brown's letter was being prepared.

1 February 2013

⇨ The above information is reprinted courtesy of *The Staffordshire Sentinel*. Please visit www.thisisstaffordshire.co.uk for further information.

© The Staffordshire Sentinel 2013

The harsh realities of 'being raped for a living'

A former Dublin prostitute speaks about her seven years working in the Irish sex trade and argues against the idea that legalisation can make the work any safer.

Following the latest revelations about Ireland's booming prostitution rackets, a former Dublin prostitute has written a stark account of her seven-year ordeal in the industry which began when she was just 15.

At that young age, circumstances no child should ever experience forced her to sell her body to elderly men, who would openly be aroused by abusing a child. Before she managed to extricate herself from a life in which she says she was 'raped for a living', she admits she even contemplated suicide...

'The nation is finally beginning to take a look at the intrinsic harm of prostitution. I welcome this because it is a harm I have understood since I was a 15-year-old prostitute, being used by up to ten men a day. The one thing that linked those men together, besides their urges to pay to abuse my young body, was that they all knew just how young I was. They all knew because I told them, and I told them because it had the near-universal effect of causing them to become very aroused.

"Under Irish law, the abusive nature of prostitution has been allowed to flourish unhindered and it is a living hell for the women struggling to survive within it"

'When a man is very aroused in street prostitution that is a good thing, because it means he'll climax quickly and the whole ordeal will be over fairly fast. I learned that on my very first day while sitting in the car of an elderly man who repeated over and over the thing that was causing him such sexual joy: "Oh, you're very young – aren't you? Aren't you?"

'That is the true, sleazy and debased face of prostitution – the face that pro-prostitution lobby groups hysterically deny and attempt to conceal. Well, they cannot conceal it from me. I spent too long looking at it, too long being abused by it, and too long trying to recover from the soul-level injury it left behind.

'Many of the girls I worked alongside were not much older than I was, and one was only 13 years old – and there was no shortage of grown men paying to abuse her. Most of the older women had been working since they were our age or younger, and many of them had histories of sexual abuse that predated their prostitution lives. When a person looks at a 30- or 40-something prostitute what they forget is that they are looking, in most cases, at a woman who has been inured to bodily invasion since she was a prepubescent child.

'I didn't just work outdoors. When the Sexual Offences Act of 1993 came into force it drove me and many others indoors, where we had even less autonomy over the conditions of our own lives. In the brothels and the 'escort' agencies, we had to endure the same things we did on the streets, but we had to endure them for longer, and with no screening process as to who would pay to abuse us.

'You might wonder, "if you were a prostitute, what did it matter who it was?" That is an innocent question, and it is deserving of an answer. It mattered because, far from being unaware of the abusive nature of prostitution, a lot of men were not only aware of it but actively got off on it. The misogyny from a lot of men was so potent and so deliberate it could cause nothing but trauma. And we, as the prostituted class that we were, could do nothing to protect ourselves other than try to avoid its most potent manifestations. This had been at least somewhat possible on the streets, where we could do our best to discern whether or not a man had hatred and the desire to hurt us seeping out of every pore. It was not at all possible once we'd gotten run indoors, and the immediate effect was a rapid escalation in violence and murder.

"The nation is finally beginning to take a look at the intrinsic harm of prostitution"

'Irish prostitution has been mainly conducted indoors since then, and nothing about this ugliness has abated because it's been concealed from the public view. In fact the opposite has been true. We were abused more thoroughly, not less, with the only difference being that now there was the secrecy of closed doors to conceal it.

'There is no doubt that many of these men had daughters older than I was, yet the abuse they unleashed on me was devastating, violent, humiliating and degrading. It was paid sexual abuse. It was ritualistic, and I experienced it in every area of prostitution.

'Do not for a moment think that the men paying to abuse here are not 'ordinary men'. I could not count the number of wedding rings and babies car seats I encountered. The men who pay to debase and degrade women and girls in prostitution are the same men who play out the pretence of being happily married family men. I wonder sometimes at the amount of women who would be shocked, not only to know their husbands are visiting prostitutes, but also to know the depth of their own husbands' contempt and misogynistic hatred of women.

'Under Irish law, the abusive nature of prostitution has been allowed to flourish unhindered and it is a living hell for the women struggling to survive within it. It is primarily for the sake of these women, but also for all of us who want to live in a gender-equal society, that I am gladdened to see the Irish Government finally pledge to tackle this issue.

'I only hope that they go the right way about it, which is to criminalise the purchase of sex, because nothing will change for prostituted women and girls until the commercialisation of female bodies is dealt the hammer-blow it so richly deserves.

'To those who would say legalisation would make prostitution safer: I think the same thing any former prostitute I've ever spoken to thinks, which is that you may as well legalise rape and battery to try to make them safer. You cannot legislate away the dehumanising, degrading trauma of prostitution, and if you try to, you are accepting a separate class of women should exist who have no access to the human rights everyone else takes for granted.'

15 February 2012

⇨ The above article originally appeared in the printed version of the *Irish Examiner*. Please visit www.turnofftheredlight.ie for further information.

© *Irish Examiner*

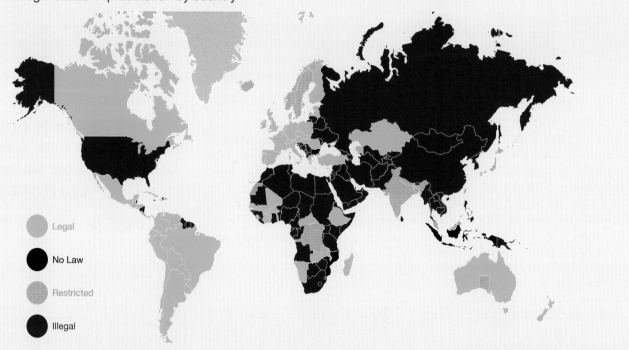

The legal status of prostitution by country

Legal

No Law

Restricted

Illegal

This map shows the legal status of prostitution (not activities surrounding prostitution such as brothels, pimping, etc.) by country. Prostitution is engaging in sexual activity with another person in exchange for compensation, such as money or other valuable goods.

Number of countries prostitution is illegal: 109
Number of countries prostitution is restricted: 11
Number of countries prostitution is legal: 77
Number of countries with no laws for prostitution: 5
The legal status of prostitution varies from country to country, from being legal and considered a profession to being punishable by death. In some jurisdictions prostitution is illegal. In other places prostitution itself (exchanging sex for money) is legal, but most surrounding activities such as soliciting in a public place, operating a brothel and other forms of pimping are illegal, often making it very difficult to engage in prostitution without breaking any law. In a few jurisdictions prostitution is legal and regulated.

Sources

Bureau of Democracy, Human Rights, and Labor 2009, Human Rights Reports, 2009, The U.S. State Department, United States, viewed 30th March, 2010, <http://www.state.gov/g/drl/rls/hrrpt/index.htm>.

INTERPOL 2009, Legislation of INTERPOL member states on sexual offences against children, 2009, INTERPOL, France, viewed 30th March, 2010, <http://www.interpol.int/Public/Children/SexualAbuse/NationalLaws/Default.asp>.

prostitution.procon.org 2010, 100 Countries and Their Prostitution Policies, 2010, ProCon.org, Online, viewed 30th March, 2010, <http://prostitution.procon.org/view.resource.php?resourceID=000772>.

New Internationalist 1994, PROSTITUTION - Prostitution & The Law - The FACTS, issue 252, New Internationalist Publications Ltd, UK, viewed 30th March, 2010, <http://www.newint.org/issue252/facts.htm>.

SWAN 2008, The Netherlands: What is the future of Amsterdam's Red Light District?, 2008, Sex Workers Rights Advocacy Network, Online, viewed 30th March, 2010, <http://swannet.org/en/node/904>.

Panama Legal 2010, Crime and Safety in Panama, 2010, Panama Legal, S.A., Guatemala, viewed 30th March, 2010, <http://www.panamalaw.org/panama_crime_and_safety.html>.

East Timor Law Journal 2004, SOCIAL PROBLEMS IN EAST TIMOR - POLICY AND LEGISLATIVE CONSIDERATIONS. METHODOLOGICAL ANALYSES TOWARDS DEMOCRATIC TRANSFORMATION IN EAST TIMOR: RESEARCH REPORTS BY CIVIL SOCIETY, 2003 - 2004, East Timor Law Journal, Online, viewed 30th March, 2010, <http://www.eastimorlawjournal.org/ROCCIPI_Analysis_East_Timor_Social_Problems/Index.html>.

IGLHRC 1996, Uruguay: Parliament Considers Legalization of Prostitution, 1996, International Gay & Lesbian Human Rights Commission, New York, NY, viewed 30th March, 2010, <http://www.iglhrc.org/cgi-bin/iowa/article/takeaction/resourcecenter/60.html>.

Ministry of Justice 2003, Prostitution Reform Act 2003, 2003, Ministry of Justice, New Zealand Legislation, viewed 2nd January, 2011, <http://www.legislation.govt.nz/act/public/2003/0028/latest/DLM197815.html>.

The above information is reprinted with kind permission from ChartsBin. Please visit www.chartsbin.com/view/snb for further information. © ChartsBin.com 2013

Citation: ChartsBin statistics collector team 2010, The Legal Status of Prostitution by Country, ChartsBin.com, viewed 5th February, 2013, <http://chartsbin.com/view/snb>.

Legalised prostitution increases human trafficking

Countries where prostitution is legal experience larger reported inflows of human trafficking, according to new research that investigates the impact of legalised prostitution on what is thought to be one of the fastest growing criminal industries in the world.

Every year, thousands of men, women and children are trafficked across international borders. The vast majority of countries in the world are affected by trafficking, whether as a country of origin, transit or destination for victims. The United Nations estimated in 2008 that nearly 2.5 million people from 127 different countries had been being trafficked into 137 countries around the world.

Research on human trafficking is still in its early stages, but is growing as the seriousness of the problem becomes more apparent. It is thought to be second only to drug trafficking as the most profitable illegal industry.

The article, *Does Legalized Prostitution Increase Human Trafficking?*, by Professor Eric Neumayer of the London School of Economics and Political Science (LSE), Dr Seo-Young Cho of the German Institute for Economic Research, and Professor Axel Dreher of Heidelberg University, is due to be published in the January 2013 edition of the journal *World Development*.

Describing international human trafficking as 'one of the dark sides of globalisation', it explains that most victims of international human trafficking are women and girls, the vast majority of whom end up being sexually exploited through prostitution. Domestic policy on prostitution in countries of destination, it says, has a marked effect.

The researchers used a global sample of 116 countries. They found that countries where prostitution is legal tend to experience a higher reported inflow of human trafficking than countries in which prostitution is prohibited.

The article's authors also looked in more detail at Sweden, Germany and Denmark, which changed their prostitution laws during the past 13 years. Sweden prohibited it in 1999, while Germany further legalised it by allowing third-party involvement in 2002. Denmark decriminalised it in 1999 so that self-employed prostitution is legal, but brothel operation is still forbidden.

Germany showed a sharp increase in reports of human trafficking upon fully legalising prostitution in 2002. The number of human trafficking victims in 2004 in Denmark, where it is decriminalised, was more than four times that of Sweden, where it is illegal, although the population size of Sweden is about 40 per cent larger.

Eric Neumayer, Professor of Environment and Development at LSE, commented: 'Most victims of international human trafficking are women and girls coerced into the sex industry abroad. We wanted to find out if legalised prostitution increases or reduces demand for trafficked women. One theory is that legalised prostitution reduces demand because legally residing prostitutes are favoured over trafficked ones after legalisation. However, our research suggests that in countries where prostitution is legalised, there is such a significant expansion of the prostitution market that the end result is larger reported inflows of human trafficking. While legalising prostitution can have positive effects on the working conditions of those legally employed in the industry, it also appears to boost the market for this fast-growing global criminal industry.'

The researchers warn that due to the clandestine nature of both trafficking and prostitution markets, their analysis had to rely on the best available existing data on reported human trafficking inflows. That legalised prostitution increases human trafficking inflows is likely, but cannot be proven with available evidence. The researchers also note that other reasons might speak against prohibiting prostitution despite its impact on human trafficking.

The article concludes: 'The likely negative consequences of legalised prostitution on a country's inflows of human trafficking might be seen to support those who argue in favour of banning prostitution, thereby reducing the flows of trafficking. However, such a line of argumentation overlooks potential benefits that the legalisation of prostitution might have on those employed in the industry. Working conditions could be substantially improved for prostitutes – at least those legally employed – if prostitution is legalised. Prohibiting prostitution also raises tricky 'freedom of choice' issues concerning both the potential suppliers and clients of prostitution services.'

5 December 2012

⇨ The above article is reprinted with kind permission from the London School of Economics. Please visit www.lse.ac.uk for further information.

What is sex trafficking?

Sex trafficking is the exploitation of people, usually women and children, within national or across international borders for the purposes of forced prostitution.

The United Nations defines trafficking as:

'The recruitment, transportation, transfer, harbouring or receipt of persons, by means of the threat or use of force or other forms of coercion, of abduction, of fraud, of deception, of the abuse of power or of a position of vulnerability or of the giving or receiving of payments or benefits to achieve the consent of a person having control over another person, for the purpose of exploitation.'

There are two distinct types of trafficking – trafficking for the purpose of sexual exploitation or forced prostitution, i.e. sex trafficking – and trafficking for the purpose of forced labour.

What's the difference between sex trafficking and people smuggling?

Human trafficking and people smuggling are often confused, but are quite different phenomena. Smuggling differs in a number of key ways. It involves:

⇨ Travel: involves transportation from one country to another, where legal entry would be denied upon arrival at the international border.

⇨ Choice: people voluntarily request or hire an individual, known as a smuggler, to covertly transport them from one location to another. There may be no deception involved in the (illegal) agreement.

⇨ Freedom: after entry into the country and arrival at their ultimate destination, the smuggled person is usually free to find their own way.

By contrast, human trafficking victims:

⇨ Are not necessarily moved. Human trafficking does not require the physical movement of a person.

⇨ Are forced to work or provide services to the trafficker or others.

⇨ Are not permitted to leave upon arrival at their destination. They are held against their will through acts of coercion.

Who are the victims?

The overwhelming majority of people trafficked are women and children.

Human trafficking affects virtually every region in the world. Estimates show that between 700,000 and four million women and children are trafficked each year worldwide for forced labour, domestic servitude or sexual exploitation.

Trafficking victims tend to be the poorest and most vulnerable, such as homeless individuals, runaway teens, displaced homemakers, refugees and drug addicts.

Where are victims from?

The United Kingdom (UK) is a destination country for men, women and children trafficked from Africa, Asia and Eastern Europe (US State Department, 2010).

Victims are also from the UK, particularly children who are trafficked internally for the purpose of prostitution.

Inadequate protection measures for these victims can result in their re-trafficking throughout the UK.

Why does sex trafficking exist?

The 'push' factor

While factors such as gender discrimination, organised crime syndicates, conflict and regional natural disasters all contribute greatly to the increase of sex trafficking within a particular area, the single greatest contributing factor to sex trafficking is poverty.

In countries where women cannot work because of a depressed economy and therefore a lack of employment opportunities:

⇨ many are attracted by the lure of fraudulent employment opportunities overseas

⇨ some will turn to prostitution as a means to feed themselves and their families

⇨ families may sell their young daughters to traffickers because they are so desperate for money.

Sometimes girls are aware to some degree they will be expected to work in the sex industry, but are so desperate to lift themselves and their families out of poverty

that they are willing to risk the consequences – although they never anticipate the abusive or coercive circumstances they find themselves in from which escape may be both difficult and dangerous.

The 'pull' factor

The 'pull' factor is the demand for sexual services that create the need for a 'supply' of trafficked women and girls. Receiving or destination countries are those with sex industries that create the demand for women to be used in prostitution.

There has been relatively little analysis of the 'demand' side of sex trafficking to date, although this gap in research is starting to be addressed.

Governments play a key role in either suppressing or fuelling the flow of women and children for commercial sexual exploitation depending on their policies on immigration and/or the sex industry.

Efforts to curb the demand side of sex trafficking may include:

⇨ education and treatment programmes for men who purchase sex

⇨ the criminalisation of those purchasing sex

⇨ community efforts to reduce demand

⇨ awareness and prevention programmes.

What's it like to be a victim of sex trafficking?

It is deeply harmful to the women and girls who are victims of trafficking.

Beyond the physical abuse, they often suffer acute depression and post-traumatic stress disorder. Many turn to alcohol and drugs to deal with the mental and physical effects of sex trafficking.

Research into the effects of trafficking found nearly eight in every ten women (76%) had been physically assaulted by traffickers, pimps, madams, brothel and club owners, clients, or their boyfriends (London School of Tropical Hygiene, 2006).

Respondents described being:

⇨ kicked while pregnant

⇨ burned with cigarettes

⇨ hit with bats or other objects

⇨ dragged across the room by their hair

⇨ punched in the face

⇨ having their head slammed against floors or walls.

90% had been physically forced or intimidated into sex or doing something sexual.

89% reported receiving threats including threats of death, beatings, increased debt, harm to their children and families or threats of re-trafficking.

Who traffics people and how?

Traffickers may be members of highly sophisticated networks of organised crime, but they may equally be family members or friends of the trafficked victim.

Trafficked victims may themselves be used later on to traffick other women and children.

Traffickers will typically exploit vulnerabilities and lack of opportunities, while offering promises of marriage, employment, education, and/or an overall better life to women and girls.

They may use deceit, coercion, force, abduction, abuse of powers, threats, or any combination of these to trick or manipulate the trafficking victim into sexual exploitation.

Trafficking is an extremely lucrative industry – the total annual revenue for trafficking in persons is estimated to be between USD$5 billion and $9 billion.

What support exists for survivors of sex trafficking?

In theory, states have a duty of care to survivors of sex trafficking.

In May 2005 the Council of Europe formally adopted the Convention on Action against Trafficking in Human Beings, which provides for legal protection and minimum standards of care for individuals who have been victims of human trafficking.

The legal protection and minimum standards of care for victims includes the following:

⇨ A minimum recovery and reflection period

⇨ Temporary residence permits for those who may be in danger if they return to their country of origin

⇨ Temporary residence permits for children if it is in their best interests to remain in the UK

⇨ Access to specialist support, emergency medical care, legal advice and the provision of safe housing.

The Convention has been signed by the United Kingdom and measures were put in place to adopt the protection for the victims of human trafficking in 2009.

The UK Human Trafficking Centre has also been created to ensure that the obligations under the Convention are adhered to.

However, these measures are inadequate. In 2010 a group of anti-trafficking organisations, the Anti-Trafficking Monitoring Group, found that:

⇨ The UK's new anti-trafficking measures are not 'fit for purpose'

⇨ The Government is breaching its obligations under the European Convention against Trafficking

⇨ The National Referral System to deal with victims of trafficking is flawed

⇨ Victims are still dealt with by UK Border Agency Staff who reportedly put more emphasis on the immigration status of the presumed trafficked persons than on the alleged crime against them.

What's it got to do with me?

Sex trafficking is a horrific crime that needs to be stopped.

It persists because it is hidden from view.

It will only end when people act to:

⇨ Expose the sexual exploitation of vulnerable human beings

⇨ Challenge the demand for sexual services that fuels the need for a supply of trafficked women and girls

⇨ Tackle the poverty and inequality that force women and girls into the hands of traffickers

⇨ Prosecute the traffickers.

⇨ The above information is reprinted with kind permission from the Anti Trafficking Alliance. Please visit www.atalliance.org.uk for further information.

© 2013 Anti Trafficking Alliance

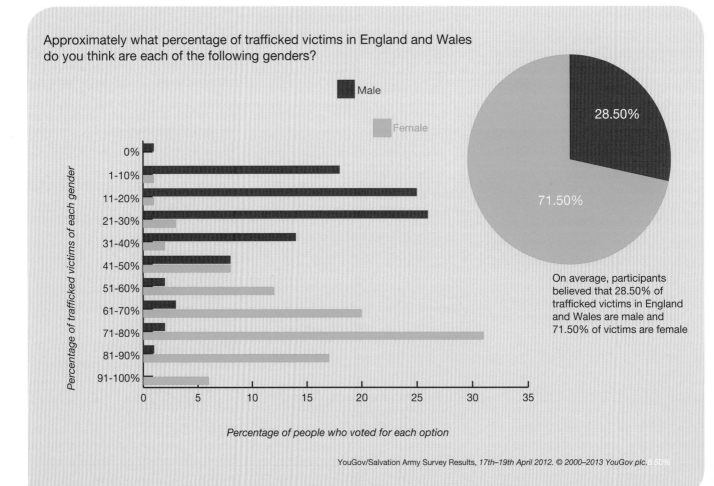

Approximately what percentage of trafficked victims in England and Wales do you think are each of the following genders?

■ Male
■ Female

Percentage of trafficked victims of each gender

0%
1-10%
11-20%
21-30%
31-40%
41-50%
51-60%
61-70%
71-80%
81-90%
91-100%

Percentage of people who voted for each option

28.50%
71.50%

On average, participants believed that 28.50% of trafficked victims in England and Wales are male and 71.50% of victims are female

YouGov/Salvation Army Survey Results, *17th–19th April 2012. © 2000–2013 YouGov plc.*

Sex trafficking and prostitution

How does sex trafficking relate to prostitution?

There is a clear link between sex trafficking and prostitution. The demand for paid sexual services creates:

⇨ The need for a supply of trafficked women

⇨ The opportunity for criminal gangs to make money from trafficking women to meet that need.

We therefore believe that you cannot end sex trafficking without addressing the demand for paid sexual services.

Would legalising prostitution give trafficked women more rights?

No. We believe that the legalisation of prostitution would increase the proliferation of sex trafficking, because it promotes the view of prostitution as a victimless crime and 'normalises' the purchase of sexual favours for money.

So would you criminalise men who buy sex from women?

Yes. We believe new legislation is needed to criminalise men who buy sex from women in the UK. In Britain, it is currently not unlawful to pay for sex and this creates a market for sex trafficking.

Criminalising the purchase of sexual acts, such as has been proven to work in the Nordic European states, will help tackle sex trafficking in a number of ways:

⇨ It gives a clear message that the exploitation of women is unacceptable

⇨ It destroys the market for sex trafficking

⇨ It allows the prosecution service to use the testimony of punters to prosecute sex traffickers and so takes the burden of truth away from the sex trafficking survivor

⇨ It makes those causing harm accountable for their actions

⇨ It decriminalises those who sell sex acts whilst offering support services to exit prostitution.

Are people aware of the harm they cause by paying for sex?

Many men would not pay for sex if they knew the harm they were creating by fuelling sex trafficking and that their acts are perpetuating rape, violence and slavery.

We need to ensure that people are aware of the realities of sex trafficking and its causes and consequences so that we can all make an informed choice.

But prostitution is the oldest profession in the world – you will never end it.

Just because something has been around for a long time does not mean it's a good thing. Slavery was a legal trade for many years, but the international community took a stand against it. Sex trafficking is a modern-day form of slavery that must also be stopped.

How will these women earn a living if these men stop paying for sex with them?

Trafficked women don't receive the money that exchanges hands for their sexual services. This money goes directly to their traffickers and exploiters. The women themselves are kept as prisoners, their passports are confiscated and they are forced to sleep with as many as 50 men a day for nothing.

What about women who choose to work in prostitution?

We understand that some women will and do choose to work in prostitution and we respect their right to do this and to organise for better rights.

However, for the vast majority of women working in prostitution, and particularly trafficked women who are coerced or forced, they do not have a choice.

⇨ The above information is reprinted with kind permission from the Anti Trafficking Alliance. Please visit www.atalliance.org.uk for further information.

Child sexual exploitation explained

Child sexual exploitation is a hugely distressing, but fairly rare form of sexual, emotional and physical abuse of children.

It can be extremely difficult to recognise, as many of the warning signs are symptomatic of challenges that all parents of adolescent or near-adolescent children face. Pace recognises this, and encourages parents who are worried about their child to talk through their fears with us. The expertise that Pace offers is based on the experiences of the 600 parents who have worked with us over the last 17 years. So Pace understands for parents, the reality of child sexual exploitation is more complicated than formal definitions allow for.

As a rough guide, however, child sexual exploitation can be defined in the following terms:

⇨ It can be useful to think of child sexual exploitation as a course of conduct rather than an isolated incident. It involves relationships based on a deliberate imbalance of power.

⇨ A person under 18 is sexually exploited when they are coerced into sexual activities by one or more person(s) who have deliberately targeted their youth and inexperience in order to exercise power over them.

⇨ The process often involves a stage of 'grooming', in which the child receives gifts (such as a mobile phone, clothes, drugs or alcohol) prior to or as a result of performing sexual activities, or having sexual activities performed on them. Although every case is different, there are different models of grooming.

⇨ Child sexual exploitation may occur through the use of technology without the child's consent or immediate recognition; for example, through being persuaded to post sexual images over the Internet or through mobile phone images.

⇨ Child sexual exploitation is often conducted with actual violence or the threat of violence. This may be threatened towards the child, or her or his family and may prevent the child from disclosing the abuse, or exiting the cycle of exploitation. Indeed, the child may be so confused by the process, that they do not perceive any abuse at all.

Again, it is important to stress that most children in the UK do not encounter child sexual exploitation. If, however, your child is affected, then it is also important to remember:

⇨ It is not your fault. A child who is sexually exploited outside of its family does not indicate that their parents have neglected them, as all children are vulnerable by virtue of their age.

⇨ You are not alone – many parents have gone through what you are going through and understand your pain.

Who is responsible for CSE?

Perpetrators of child sexual exploitation come from all ages and backgrounds and both sexes, although the majority are men. Children may be sexually exploited by an individual, or by a group of people connected through formal networks (i.e. through trade, business or other community networks) or more informal friendship groups. Children are also sexually exploited by gangs with criminal associations. In these cases, the gang may benefit financially from the sexual exploitation.

Spotting the signs

Adolescence is a time of necessary experimentation and can be a particularly challenging period for the parent-child relationship.

Most parents understand the value of young people learning about themselves through new experiences, but simultaneously want to protect their child from harm.

Child sexual exploitation is a particularly insidious form of harm because it occurs only after a child has been persuaded that the sexual activities are a 'normal' part of adult life, or an 'exciting' opportunity which confirms their maturity and independence. This inevitably means a greater effort on the part of the child to conceal their actions from you. The perpetrators are both skilled and strategic; they aim to drive a wedge between you and your child, closing down the normal channels of communication and emotional bond between you both.

If you are worried and suspect that your child is grappling with something bigger than the usual ups and downs of adolescence, then there are warning signs. Many of these are typical of all teenagers, so need to be treated with caution. As a (very) general rule, we would recommend escalating your concerns if your child is exhibiting three or more of the following warning signs:

⇨ Your child may become especially secretive and stop engaging with usual friends. They may be particularly prone to sharp mood swings; many parents come to Pace reporting that their child seems to have acquired an entirely different personality. Whilst mood swings are common to all adolescents, it is the severity of behavioural change that is most indicative here.

⇨ They may be associating with, or develop a sexual relationship with older men and/or women (although bear in mind that the perpetrators often approach the child through a peer from school who is already being exploited, or through the youngest member of the grooming network).

⇨ They may go missing from home – and be defensive about their location and activities, often returning home late or staying out all night (again, perpetrators know that parents will immediately suspect something is wrong if their child stays out all night, so they may initially drop the child off at the home address and before their curfew. They may even pick them up outside the school gates).

⇨ They may receive odd calls and messages on their mobiles or social media pages from unknown, possibly much older associates from outside their normal social network.

⇨ They may be in possession of new, expensive items which they couldn't normally afford, such as mobile phones, iPods or jewellery.

⇨ Exhibit a sudden change in dressing patterns or musical taste.

⇨ Look tired and/or unwell, and sleep at unusual hours.

⇨ Have marks or scars on their body which they try to conceal.

⇨ Adopt new 'street language' or respond to a new street name.

⇨ The above information is reprinted with kind permission from Parents Against Child Sexual Exploitation (Pace). Please visit www.paceuk.info for further information.

Child sex trafficking in UK on the rise with even younger victims targeted

White, black and Asian children at risk with abusers using mobiles and web to groom victims, say Barnardo's.

By Alexandra Topping

The trafficking of British children around UK cities for sexual exploitation is on the increase with some as young as ten being groomed by predatory abusers, a report reveals today.

The average age of victims of such abuse has fallen from 15 to about 13 in five years, according to the report by Barnardo's, the UK's biggest children's charity.

But victims continue to be missed as telltale signs are overlooked 'from the frontline of children's services to the corridors of Whitehall,' said Anne Marie Carrie, the charity's new chief executive.

'Wherever we have looked for exploitation, we have found it. But the real tragedy is we believe this is just the tip of the iceberg,' she said.

Calling for a minister to be put in charge of the Government's response, she said: 'Without a minister

with overall responsibility the Government response is likely to remain inadequate.'

The main findings from the report, called *Puppet on a String*, include:

⇨ Trafficking becoming more common and sexual exploitation more organised.

⇨ Grooming methods becoming more sophisticated as abusers use a range of technology – mobile phones, including texts and picture messages, plus technology, and the Internet – to control and abuse children.

The charity dealt with 1,098 children who had been groomed for sex last year, a 4% increase on the previous year.

A recent focus on the ethnicity of abusers risks putting more children in danger, said Carrie. 'I am not going to say that ethnicity is not an issue in some geographical areas, it clearly is. But to think of it as the only determining factor is misleading and dangerous.'

The issue has come under the spotlight after cases in Derby, where ringleaders of a gang of Asian men were jailed for grooming girls as young as 12 for sex, and in Rochdale, where nine mainly Asian men were arrested on Tuesday last week on suspicion of grooming a group of white teenage girls.

Carrie warned of the risk of the issue becoming dangerously simplified after comments from the former home secretary Jack Straw, who said some Pakistani men saw white girls as 'easy meat'.

The charity dealt with white, black and Asian victims, she said – whose voices were being lost. 'Profiling and stereotyping is dangerous – we are scared that victims will say: 'I don't fit into that pattern, so I'm not being abused'.'

The report identifies many different patterns of abuse, ranging from inappropriate relationships to organised networks of child trafficking.

Of Barnardo's 22 specialist services surveyed for the report, 21 had seen evidence of the trafficking of children through organised networks for sex, often with multiple men.

Among the cases highlighted is Emma, who met her first 'boyfriend' when she was 14. In his 30s, he bought her presents, said he loved her, then forced her to have sex with his friends. She was shipped around the country and raped by countless men. 'I got taken to flats, I don't know where they were and men would be brought to me. I was never given any names, and I don't remember their faces,' she said.

The 'inappropriate relationship' usually involved an older abuser with control over a child. Such cases included Sophie, who was 13 when she met her 'gorgeous' 18-year-old boyfriend at a cousin's 21st birthday party. After initially treating her well, he isolated her from her family and became violent. When police rescued her, they told her the man was 34, with a criminal record for child abuse. 'I said they were lying. I thought I was in love, I thought it was normal,' she said.

The 'boyfriend' model, sees girls groomed, often by a younger man, who passes her on to older men. In one case an Asian teenager from the north-west described being dragged out of a car by her hair by her 'boyfriend', who took her to a hotel room 'to have his friends over and do what they wanted to me'.

Boys are also vulnerable: a 14-year-old, Tim, was groomed by one man then expected to have sex with many more. 'After a while there would be three or four guys all at once. It was horrible and very scary,' he said.

Abusers are increasingly using the Internet and mobile phone technology to control victims. Teens are being coerced into sending, or posing for, sexually explicit photos which are then used to blackmail and control them, said Carrie. 'The abuser then sells the images, and threatens to send the pictures to the girl's parents or school if she does not do x, y and z.'

Often abusers target the most vulnerable: children in care, foster homes or from chaotic backgrounds. But children of all backgrounds are at risk, said Carrie.

Penny Nicholls, director of children and young people at The Children's Society, said the Barnardo's findings echoed their experiences. 'We join Barnardo's in calling on the Government to take urgent action, ensuring a minister has special responsibility for overseeing a countrywide response to combat sexual exploitation.'

A Department for Education spokeswoman said: 'This is a complex problem and we are determined to tackle it effectively by working collaboratively right across government and with national and local agencies.'

17 January 2011

⇨ The article originally appeared in *The Guardian* and is reprinted with permission. Please visit www.guardian.co.uk for further information.

© 2013 Guardian News & Media Limited

Prostitution, trafficking and sexual exploitation support services

Number of PTSE Services

● 0

● 1

● 2

● 3-5

Data sources:
Services and Projects data supplied
by CWASU, London Metropolitan University

Local Authority Digital Boundaries used
under licensefrom UKBorders,
an EDINA service

Glasgow

Newcastle upon Tyne

Leeds

Manchester

Nottingham

Walsall

London

Map of prostitution, trafficking and sexual exploitation support services UK, *the Equality and Human Rights Commission (the EHRC).* © EHRC 2013

* The copyright and all other intellectual property rights in the Map of prostitution, trafficking and sexual exploitation support services in the UK are owned by, or licensed to, the Commission for Equality and Human Rights, known as the Equality and Human Rights Commission ("the EHRC")

Oxford child trafficking: 13 suspects arrested for prostitution of young girls

Detectives believe they have smashed a child trafficking gang preying on runaways as young as 11 for Britain's sex trade.

13 men were arrested in Oxford by police investigating claims 24 vulnerable girls under 16 were groomed for rape.

Officers suspect gang members targeted children in care or living rough and transported them around Britain over a six-year period.

Amid fears more children may be involved, patrols of officers took to the streets of the university city to hand out public awareness leaflets.

Thames Valley Police said nine men – aged between 21 and 37 – remain in custody and are being quizzed over a string of offences including causing the prostitution of females under the age of 18, administering drugs for the purpose of rape, trafficking, grooming and rape.

Four men, aged 23, 31, 34 and 37, were released on bail until 19 April.

Police became aware of the allegations after a number of girls were reported missing.

Detective Superintendent Rob Mason said: 'We believe we have uncovered an organised crime group who have been running a business of selling young girls for sex.

'We have also identified a number of customers who we have reason to believe have used this service.'

More than 100 officers took part in raids as the force executed 14 warrants across the city as part of an operation named Bullfinch.

Police were not willing to comment on the nationalities of any of the suspects but sources said many of the offences centred in or around the Oxford area.

Many of the alleged victims were said to have been 'known' to children's services.

Mason, speaking later at the force's city headquarters, said the inquiry was still at an early stage.

'We consider the girls to be very, very vulnerable and that's why they have been targeted,' Mr Mason said.

'The girls have gone missing and when they returned they have made certain disclosures.

'Through children's services and Oxfordshire County Council we have become aware of some of the activities the girls have been getting into when they've gone missing.'

Police suspect they have arrested both those behind the running of the network and the men that have paid for sex.

The officer added: 'The investigation has been very challenging. The girls are very vulnerable and a number of them do not consider themselves to be victims.'

Detectives are keeping an 'open mind' as to whether there would be further arrests.

'It is going to be a long investigation,' Mason added. 'Our priority is the welfare of the girls.'

Much of yesterday's activity was centred near St Aldates police station in central Oxford. More than 40 uniformed officers and community support officers were handing out A5 flyers about the operation.

Police chiefs also posted a video on YouTube to reassure community members and urge any potential victims to come forward.

Officers are working closely with children's services, the Child Exploitation and Online Protection Centre and other forces that have been through similar investigations.

Police are also urging anyone who thinks they may have been a victim to contact ChildLine on 0800 1111.

23 March 2012

⇨ The above article is reprinted with kind permission from the Press Association. Please visit their website www.pressassociation.com for further information.

- ANOTHER NICE LITTLE EARNER...

Celia and Mike's story

'Our daughter changed forever when she was just 13. She had always been a rather quiet child, and we were very family orientated. We worked hard to cultivate family values and taught our children to respect them.

But one day we received a call from her school. They were concerned because Kitty had started hanging around with a certain group of girls. We were advised that these girls could be a bad influence. We spoke to our daughter, but because she did not form friendships easily and was naturally shy, she was not dissuaded from parting with her new gang of friends. When we invited these girls round for tea, she told us that she had to go to their houses, as their mothers worked in the evenings and they had younger siblings.

"We gasped as she told them that the men had given her vodka and cigarettes"

As she turned 14, Kitty started to go to the cinema or on shopping trips at the weekend – all normal teenage activities. When the school told us she had been missing the odd lesson, she swore to us she only ever missed PE. But the alarm bells kept ringing when she gradually changed her appearance. Suddenly she was wearing tracksuits and expensive trainers, scrunching her hair up tightly and wearing large earrings. Her taste in music changed from boybands to baseline.

Then one night, the police turned up at midnight, asking to speak to Kitty. One of her friends had been reported missing, shortly after Kitty had been seen with her. As she rubbed her eyes in her pink pyjamas and fluffy dressing gown, the police fired questions at her. Where had she been that evening?

To our astonishment, Kitty told them that she had been picked up with two other girls by two men and driven round in their blue Audi. We gasped as she told them that the men had given her vodka and cigarettes, then dropped her back home at her normal curfew of 8:30pm, and driven off again. The police then told us that the men were known groomers. Neither my husband or I knew what this meant, but a cold chill gripped my heart as the officer explained how young girls were being befriended then sexually exploited by groups of men.

Eventually we got in touch with the parents of one of her girlfriends. They passed on details for the Missing Persons Coordinator and a number for Pace. For the first time we realised we were not alone and we able to share our burden with people who understood. Pace workers listened to us, and we met other parents through parent support groups.

Kitty became more and more distanced from us. We tried locking the doors and hiding the keys. Once, when she started scrambling out of a window, I even called the police and had her arrested. It was the hardest thing I have ever done in my life, but I was desperately trying to keep my daughter safe. The men had manipulated her so successfully, that she only saw us as the enemy.

We were getting very little sleep from driving round all night looking for our daughter. Sometimes she would ring and ask us to pick her up from a rundown part of our city, or even from another town. It was clear that the men were giving her drugs. As a practising nurse, I recognised the dilated pupils and giddiness.

Then one night we reported her missing when she failed to return at 11pm. This time two police officers came round and returned throughout the night, until she came back in at 5:30am. She staggered in, obviously high on drugs, her neck covered in bruises and bites. One of the officers went through her phone, reading out vile texts from men. But she just stared into space.

"Only when she was punched in the stomach by one of her abusers did she finally walk away"

The next day she told us she needed to get away. She has never told us the full extent of harm she suffered from these men, but we were so determined to set her free from her evil spell that my husband took leave and took her to Spain for a few months. It seemed to work for a while, but to our horror, she gradually fell back in with the old crowd. Then, at 17 years old she became pregnant. Only when she was punched in the stomach by one of her abusers did she finally walk away.

Two years later she is caring for her beautiful son with us in our home. Our grandson is delightful and we can't imagine life without him. But what these men did to our daughter nearly destroyed our lives – including those of our other two children. Kitty still feels she is unable to live alone, but we hope the day will come when she can experience some independence and take up her education again.'

⇨ The above information is reprinted with kind permission from Parents Against Child Sexual Exploitation (Pace). Please visit www.paceuk.info for further information.

© Parents Against Child Sexual Exploitation (Pace) 2013

The silent victims of sex trafficking

By Carmen Cuesta Roca

When people discuss human trafficking, the usual stereotypical imagery is evoked: an international young woman trafficked across borders, a group of children forced to harvest distant crops, an inner city brothel exposed as exploiting dozens of young girls and women. But rarely do we read of the male victims of human trafficking. Men typically occupy the role of the perpetrator in these stories, but this does not mean that male survivors of trafficking should be denied their status as victims.

Yes, perpetrators of sex-trafficking usually target society's most vulnerable members (women and children). However, research proves that men are forming an increasingly larger percentage of the victims. An alarming statistic in a 2008 US State Department report on human trafficking reveals that between 2006 and 2008, the percentage of adult male victims of human trafficking jumped from 6% to 45%. In the UK, it's a similar story: men account for more than two-fifths (41%) of adult victims of human trafficking in England and Wales helped by the Salvation Army, contrary to the public perception that the crime almost exclusively affects women.

According to ILO and UNICEF, 2% of those forced into commercial sexual exploitation are men or boys, but the practice might be far more widespread than reported due to social stigmas associated with sex with boys. Most male victims do not report their abuse, as well as there being fewer services available to them, and virtually no concern for them either socially or from government-run organisations. A Canadian study found that sexually exploited boys were exploited at younger ages than girls, and remained in their situation longer. In addition, a US Department of State report on trafficking in Burma highlights that there were no shelter facilities available to male victims.

This lack of concern renders male victims invisible. This is evident in cases such as this article published on The Good Men Project blog, which claims its aims include the fostering of a national discussion centred around modern manhood and the question, 'What does it mean to be a good man?' The article is written by the project's founder, and despite the general title 'Sex Slavery in America', the focus remains solely on female victims throughout the article. One reader commented on the blog after having comments pulled, 'It is unfortunate that it appears that The Good Men Project does not want to acknowledge male victims of sexual exploitation, and worse that it appears to now block anyone who mentions them.'

This under-representation of male victims of sex trafficking is most definitely due to the fact that sexual violence against males is a taboo subject; it happens but it is concealed by the victims who are too ashamed to speak out, and by a society that is not prepared to listen. According to the FBI's Uniform Crime Reporting system, forcible rape is 'the carnal knowledge of a female forcibly and against her will'. To the FBI, the carnal knowledge of a male forcibly and against his will is considered a different (and lesser) crime: 'assault'. It is instances such as these that prove men can suffer just as much as women do from gendered stereotypes and power-structures.

That men do not typically fit into the role of victims as women do, is not just a reflection on the stereotypes inflicted onto women but also a portrayal of the injustices suffered by men who do not conform to society's ideal of masculinity. It is clear that more help must be offered to male victims of sexual violence, as invisible victims cannot be helped. But what is also clear is that in order to bring male victims into sight, attitudes must be adjusted and taboos need to be broken down. We need to stop being so squeamish and accept the realities that occur in our world in order to overcome them.

22 November 2012

⇨ The above information is reprinted with kind permission from *Protocol*. Please visit www.protocol-magazine.com for further information.

Key facts

- 60% of teenagers interviewed said that viewing pornography affected their self-esteem and body image. 45% of young women said they were unhappy with their breasts and would consider plastic surgery and 27% of young men were concerned about the shape and size of their penis. (page 1)

- The porn industry produces 68 million search engine requests each day. (page 2)

- A study that examined over 300 scenes from the most popular adult videos released in 2005 in the US found that 89.8% of scenes included either verbal or physical aggression. 94.4% of aggressive acts were targeted at women. (page 2)

- A study in which participants were exposed to less than five hours of pornography over a six-week period resulted in participants showing much more lenient attitudes to rapists. (page 3)

- Chlamydia and Gonorrhea infections among performers are ten times greater than that of ordinary 20–24-year-olds who are not performers. (page 3)

- 20% of all pornographic images online are of children. (page 6)

- It is illegal to buy or distribute porn if you are under 18. This means that if you lend a pornographic DVD to someone under 18, or even use Bluetooth to send them a porn clip, you are breaking the law. (page 8)

- It is illegal to make a pornographic film containing children. Anyone under 18 counts as a child. (page 8)

- 92 countries have no legislation at all that specifically addresses child pornography. (page 9)

- Approximately 73% of British households now have access to the Internet. (page 10)

- 74% of 5- to 16-year-olds have their own laptop or PC. (page 10)

- The largest group of Internet pornography consumers is children aged 12–17. (page 10)

- 61% of children aged 7–16 have a mobile phone that can access the Internet. (page 11)

- 40% of 11- to 14-year-olds have used their mobile phones or computer to send pictures of themselves or receive naked or topless images of friends. (page 11)

- 93% of women and 73% of men found that the ease with which pornographic content can be viewed on the Internet is damaging to children. (page 11)

- A report by ChildLine says that the number of calls from teenagers upset by seeing adult images has increased by 34% in the past year. (page 12)

- 75% of women involved in prostitution started as children. (page 19)

- 74% of women cite poverty as the primary motivator for entering prostitution. (page 19)

- Up to 95% of women in prostitution are problematic drug users. (page 19)

- Nine out of ten women in prostitution would like to exit if they could. (page 19)

- 68% of women in prostitution meet the criteria for Post Traumatic Stress Disorder in the same range as torture victims and combat veterans undergoing treatment. (page 19)

- Between 700,000 and four million women and children are trafficked each year worldwide for forced labour, domestic servitude or sexual exploitation. (page 31)

- The average age of victims of child sexual exploitation has fallen from 15- to 13-years-old in five years. (page 35)

- Men account for more than two-fifths (41%) of adult victims of human trafficking in England and Wales helped by the Salvation Army. (page 39)

Automatic porn filters

Some people feel that automatic porn filters are needed in order to protect people, particularly children, from viewing disturbing pornographic images online. The idea is that, on purchasing a new PC or Internet service, adults would be forced to choose which types of content they wanted to be accessed on their computer. This would mean that any site categorised as inappropriate – sites containing porn, suicide, self-harm sites, etc. – would be blocked. There is concern, however, that this could result in genuine websites being blocked unfairly, for example medical or self-help sites.

Brothel

A house where people can pay to have sex with prostitutes.

Censorship

Banning or cutting out content that is deemed 'unsuitable'. Many people argue that introducing filters to block pornography from Internet searches, would be a form of censorship. Censorship is generally viewed as a negative thing.

Child Sexual Exploitation (CSE)

Using or exploiting a child for sexual purposes. This often goes hand-in-hand with the grooming process and can involve offering the child money, gifts, cigarettes or alcohol in return for sexual favours. CSE can lead to child trafficking and prostitution.

Empower

To give power or authority to someone.

Exploitation

Taking advantage of or using someone for selfish reasons.

Grooming

Actions that are deliberately performed in order to encourage a child to engage in sexual activity. For example, offering friendship and establishing an emotional connection, buying gifts, etc.

Internet Service Provider (ISP)

A company that provides Internet services, such as BT, Talk Talk, Sky, etc.

Pornography

Images or videos that explicitly portray sexual activity.

Prostitution

The exchange of money for sex.

Rape

Forcing someone to engage in sexual intercourse against their will. Force is not necessarily physical, it could also be emotional or psychological.

Sex trafficking

Transporting people from one area to another in order to force them to work in the sex trade – usually as prostitutes, but they could be forced into the porn industry also. Sex trafficking does not just occur between countries, it also happens within the UK and is closely linked to child sexual exploitation and grooming.

Soliciting

When a prostitute searches for clients.

Assignments

1. Read the article *What is pornography?* on page 1, written by the organisation Faith Relationships & Young People (FRYP). Visit the FRYP website and make notes on the following questions: What are the FRYP's aims and objectives? Do you think these might influence the way they view pornography? Do you think their article is unbiased? Use evidence from their website and the article on page 1 to back up your ideas.

2. Create an outline for a lesson that will teach pupils from your age group about pornography. Think carefully about what you believe needs to be included in the lesson; which issues are most important? Work in groups and then present back to the rest of your class and compare ideas.

3. Do you agree with the points raised in the article *Teaching children about sex: pornography lessons in schools, anyone?* on page 14? Write a letter to the author either agreeing or disagreeing with her.

4. As a class, stage a television talk show with the theme 'Should we teach pornography in schools?' The talk show panel should include a teacher, a politician, a parent and a journalist. One member of the class should also play the part of the talk show host, fielding questions from the audience as you debate the issue. Take some time to decide who will play each part, and think about what their opinion would be.

5. Write a letter to your MP arguing either for or against an automatic block on Internet porn.

6. Look at the graphs on pages 10 and 11. Using the same questions, conduct a survey among people in your year group. Use your findings to create your own set of graphs and compare them to the ones from the London School of Economics. Are your results similar?

7. In regard to prostitution law, research The Nordic Model – how is it different from complete decriminalisation? Create a factsheet explaining the basic principles.

8. With a partner, discuss the pros and cons of completely legalising prostitution. Make notes and present your ideas back to the class.

9. Use the article on pages 21–23, *Know your rights: An A–Z for sex workers*, to create a PowerPoint presentation explaining the laws surrounding prostitution in the UK. You should also research and include proposed changes to the law.

10. Look at the graphs on page 22. What do they tell you about men's attitudes towards prostitutes? Consider the source of the figures, the dates of the survey and how the questionnaire was conducted.

11. Design a poster campaign for the London Underground system that will highlight the realities of life for women involved in prostitution. Read the articles *Prostitution – the facts* on page 19 and *The harsh realities of 'being raped for a living'* on page 27 for background information.

12. Do some research into the prevalence of prostitution in the Victorian era. What was life like for prostitutes in the 19th century? Have conditions improved for commercial sex workers over the past 150 years? Or are they worse?

13. In small groups, plan the making of a TV programme that will highlight the plight of male trafficking victims. Your programme could be either a drama or documentary. Use *The silent victims of sex trafficking* on page 39 for background information, and conduct further research.

14. Create an information booklet, to be distributed at your school, explaining sexual exploitation and highlighting the warning signs for young people who might become victims.

15. Look at the map of *prostitution, trafficking and sexual exploitation services* on page 36. Choose one of the highlighted areas and research the services available. What organisations are based in that area? What do they do? Write notes and be prepared to feedback to your class.

16. Read *Celia and Mike's Story* on page 38. Write a letter to Kitty, warning her of the dangers of her situation and suggesting where she might go for help and support.

17. Choose an illustration from *The Sex Trade* book, such as the one on page 18. What message do you think the illustrator is trying to portray with this image? How does it support the points made in the article? Is it successful?

Acknowledgements

The publisher is grateful for permission to reproduce the following material.

While every care has been taken to trace and acknowledge copyright, the publisher tenders its apology for any accidental infringement or where copyright has proved untraceable. The publisher would be pleased to come to a suitable arrangement in any such case with the rightful owner.

Chapter 1: Pornography

What is pornography? © Faith Relationships & Young People (FRYP), *Porn – the reality behind the fantasy* © Women's Support Project, *Can sex films empower women?* © Guardian News & Media Limited, *LA County introduces condom law for porn films* © Cara Acred/ Independence Educational Publishers Ltd., *How good is porn?* © 2013 AOL (UK) Limited, *Will UK law regarding online pornography be tightened?* © Contact Law, *Legal status of child pornography by country* © ChartsBin.com 2013, *Children being exposed to pornography* © Premier Christian Media Trust and Safermedia 2013, *Should we panic about pornography?* © 2012 TSL Education Ltd. *Teaching children about sex: Pornography lessons in schools, anyone?* © independent.co.uk, *Government rejects automatic porn filters* © Cara Acred.

Chapter 2: Prostitution and trafficking

What is prostitution? © 2004 – 2013 Politics.co.uk, *Prostitution – the facts* © Object 2013, *Know your rights: An A – Z of sex workers* © English Collective of Prostitutes 2013, *Men who buy sex* © Eaves, London and Prostitution Research & Education, San Francisco, *Prostitute Rita Brown calls for legalised brothels in Stoke-on-Trent* © The Staffordshire Sentinel 2013, *The harsh realities of 'being raped for a living'* © Irish Examiner, *Legalised prostitution increases human trafficking* © LSE 2012, *What is sex trafficking?* © 2013 Anti Trafficking Alliance, *Sex trafficking and prostitution* © 2013 Anti Trafficking Alliance, *Child*

sexual exploitation explained © Parents Against Child Sexual Exploitation (Pace) 2013, *Child sex trafficking in the UK on the rise with even younger victims targeted* © 2013 Guardian News & Media Limited, *Oxford child trafficking: 13 suspects arrested for prostitution of young girls* © Press Association 2012, *Celia and Mike's Story* © Parents Against Child Exploitation (Pace) 2013, *The silent victims of sex trafficking* © Protocol 2013.

Illustrations:

Pages 18, 35: Don Hatcher; pages 20, 39: Angelo Madrid; pages 33, 37: Simon Kneebone.

Images:

Cover and pages i, 26 © romkaz, page 5 © Joe Cicack, page 7 © 07_av, page 11 © Lars Ploughmann, pages 12 &13 © Kostya Kisleyko, page 30 © George Nazmi Bebawi.

Additional acknowledgements:
Editorial on behalf of Independence Educational Publishers by Cara Acred.
With thanks to the Independence team: Mary Chapman, Sandra Dennis, Christina Hughes, Jackie Staines, and Jan Sunderland.

Cara Acred
Cambridge
May 2013